SPOTLIGHT

NAVAJO &
HOPI COUNTRY

KATHLEEN BRYANT

Contents

NAVAJO & HOPI COUNTRY

NAVAJO & HOPI COUNTRY

Northeastern Arizona contains some of the loneliest yet most extraordinary acres of the Colorado Plateau, averaging between 5,000 and 7,000 feet in elevation, where sagebrush, yucca, and desert grasses march to the rims of deep canyons and mountains are dusted with snow in winter. The wide-open country is a textbook of geology. Mesas, buttes, and volcanic features from cinder cones to lava dikes thrust above the otherwise flat expanse. Badlands, scarps, and canyons reveal colorful layers of sandstone, limestone, and shale. Ninety minutes northwest of Flagstaff, the largest ponderosa pine forest in the world spreads to both rims of the Grand Canyon, the biggest gorge of them all.

Flagstaff alone could keep a curious traveler occupied for weeks, with three national monuments, some of the Southwest's best museums, a ski resort, and miles of trails leading around the 600-plus volcanic peaks that dot the skyline. But it is the indigenous cultures that truly define this part of the Four Corners. Despite almost overwhelming odds, the Navajo and Hopi tribes have maintained their traditions into the 21st century. Farming, ranching, herding, and tourism provide an income for many, and tribal artisans continue to weave rugs, carve katsina figurines, or make silver jewelry.

With the exception of Flagstaff, the larger cities on or near the reservations, including Kayenta, Window Rock, and Winslow, are not very big, and the surrounding poverty can make them as sobering as they are inviting. Yet they offer riches of experiences: shopping

© KATHLEEN BRYANT

HIGHLIGHTS

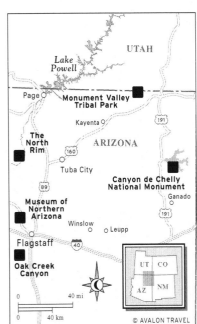

◖ Museum of Northern Arizona: An extensive collection, clearly presented, focuses on the cultural and natural history of the Colorado Plateau region (page 13).

◖ Oak Creek Canyon: Rugged cliffs shelter this recreation area between Flagstaff and Sedona, a riparian oasis of sycamores and pines, swimming holes, hiking trails, and sparkling spring-fed waters (page 27).

◖ The North Rim: Less visited and cooler in the summer, the Grand Canyon's northern rim seems a world apart from its southern one (page 35).

◖ Monument Valley Tribal Park: Towering mesas and buttes make up one of America's best-known vistas (page 46).

◖ Canyon de Chelly National Monument: A gorgeous canyon system preserves a timeless slice of Navajo life (page 49).

LOOK FOR ◖ TO FIND RECOMMENDED SIGHTS, ACTIVITIES, DINING, AND LODGING.

at trading posts and galleries; taking in breath-stopping views of Canyon de Chelly National Park, Monument Valley, or the Grand Canyon; walking the timeless villages of the Hopi Reservation. Ancestral Puebloan cliff dwellings are scattered throughout the region, with those at Navajo National Monument rivaling anything in Colorado or Utah.

Though the largest towns on the reservations have hotels, food choices and tourist services are limited, and it may be an hour or more to the next gas station. But for those who bring a sense of adventure and an open mind along with their sunscreen and hiking boots, this is a region where legend and landscape meet.

PLANNING YOUR TIME

Flagstaff makes a convenient hub for exploring northern Arizona's Indian country. The forested college town is an appealing place to spend several days, including at least a half day to peruse the collection of the outstanding **Museum of Northern Arizona.** Visiting **Grand Canyon National Park** will require at least a day, and for anything longer than a short hike, you'll need gear, permits, and some strong legs. **Sedona,** down lovely Oak Creek Canyon, is worth another day or two if you plan on soaking up some of the groovy local energy or red-rock scenery.

The Big Rez (as residents refer to the vast

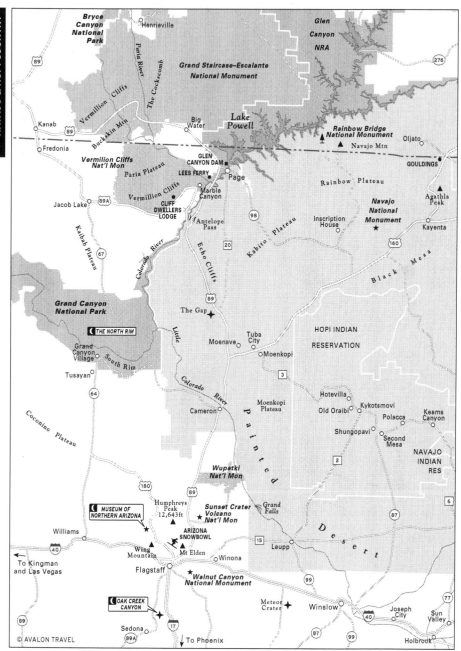

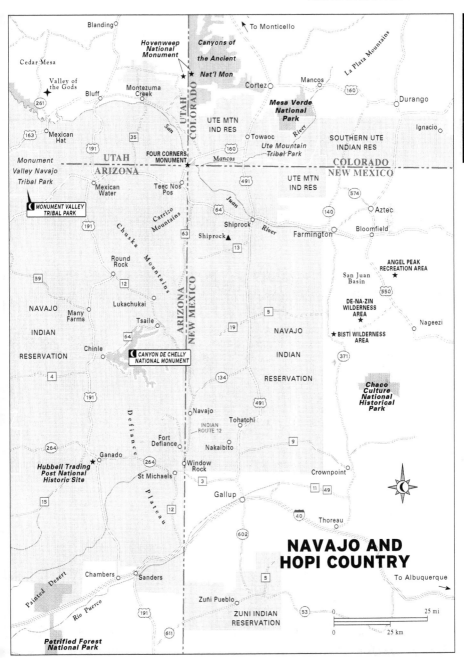

NAVAJO AND HOPI COUNTRY

Navajo Nation) has impressive attractions of its own, and each could take a day to explore. The sandy bottoms and sheer cliffs of **Canyon de Chelly** have sheltered humans for centuries. **Monument Valley** is a visual icon for good reason: The stone monoliths rising from the stark red-dirt plateau make up one of the most awesome sights in the American West. In the center of the larger Navajo Nation, the traditional Hopi villages can be explored in a day, though the motel on Second Mesa makes a pleasant overnight.

The Route 66 towns of Flagstaff, Winslow, and Holbrook lie along I-40, which parallels the southern border of the Navajo Reservation. The interstate passes the gaudy palettes of the Painted Desert and cuts through Petrified Forest National Park as it continues east to New Mexico. South of Flagstaff, I-17 leads to Phoenix. U.S. 89 runs north from Flagstaff, splitting off into U.S. 89A before reaching Page and the Utah border.

U.S. 160 leads northeast across the Navajo Reservation from Tuba City to Shiprock via Kayenta, where U.S. 163 heads north to Monument Valley and the Utah border. From Tuba City, you can also take SR 264 through the Hopi Mesas to Ganado, Window Rock, and Gallup, New Mexico. U.S. 191 travels north-south, through Ganado and Chinle to Mexican Water, Utah. Countless paved and dirt roads reach much of the rest of Indian land. Some of these tracks can be very rough, particularly in bad weather, and some are unmarked; the AAA *Guide to Indian Country* (familiar to Tony Hillerman fans as Jim Chee's map of choice) is your best weapon against getting lost.

Flagstaff and Vicinity

"Flag" (pop. 65,000) is a mountain town, and outdoor recreation centers around the ponderosa-and-aspen-covered San Francisco Peaks, which tower above the city's northern edge. It may be hard to believe as the heat waves shimmer up off the Sonoran and Mohave Deserts to the south and west, but at 7,000 feet, Flagstaff is actually the second-snowiest metropolitan area in the country after Syracuse, New York, with an average of 108 inches of snow yearly.

Flag is also a city aware of its heritage, from landmarked historical buildings to the blinking neon motel signs along Route 66. This has always been a railroad town—an average of 60 trains still roar through daily, though the city recently spent close to a million dollars to quiet the whistles downtown. Founded in 1899, Northern Arizona University (NAU) has a student population of 20,000 that helps keep the local music and art scenes lively.

Three national monuments are within a half hour of the city, which is surrounded by the Coconino National Forest. City and county parks host dozens of summertime festivals, and Lowell Observatory keeps an eye on the starry night skies year round. Skiing the Arizona Snowbowl, hiking the Grand Canyon, visiting the outstanding Museum of Northern Arizona, taking a day trip to Sedona or a nearby Indian reservation—whatever your interests, Flagstaff has plenty to offer.

History

People were living in scattered pit houses and canyon-edge dwellings in the foothills of the San Francisco Peaks when a series of eruptions from 1040 to 1100 covered 800 square miles of the surrounding countryside with lava and ash. The cinders acted as a moisture-preserving mulch, and the region's population shifted to larger pueblo-style villages that became centers of agriculture and trade. By 1250 many villagers had moved on.

After the 1848 treaty ceding Mexican lands to the United States, U.S. military engineers and surveyors explored the area, following prehistoric routes that later became wagon trails, railroads, and highways. An 1857 survey expedition was led by Lt. Edward F. Beale, whose camel corps established the Beale Road used by gold-seekers and immigrants. In 1876 a group of settlers arrived from Boston, and on July 4 they raised an American flag on a peeled pine at Antelope Springs, not far from present-day Thorpe Park. The early settlement didn't last, but the flagpole did, and travelers heading west were told to keep an eye out for the good campsite it marked.

Eventually, some settlers stayed, and so did the name Flagstaff. The post office and railroad both arrived in 1881, and by 1886 this was the biggest city on the tracks between Albuquerque and the Pacific Ocean. The Arizona Lumber and Timber Company made a fortune from the abundant forests, shipping logs out cheaply by rail. Sheep and cattle ranches provided additional jobs. Coconino County, established in 1891, was named for the Cohonina Indians, ancestors of today's Havasupai tribe.

Three years later, Percival Lowell established an observatory on a hill overlooking Flagstaff, and in 1930 Lowell Observatory astronomer Clyde Tombaugh discovered Pluto (now considered by many scientists to be a dwarf planet). In 1926 Route 66 replaced the old Beale Wagon Road and decades later was in turn replaced by I-40. The route has become a gateway for visitors discovering the wonders of the Petrified Forest, Painted Desert, the Grand Canyon, and Indian Country.

SIGHTS
San Francisco Peaks

The peaks forming Flagstaff's distinctive northern skyline were named by Spanish explorer-priests after St. Francis of Assisi, the founder of their order. The Navajos refer to the peaks as Dook'o'ooslííd ("abalone shell mountain"), the Sacred Mountain of the West. The Hopis call them Nubat-i-kyan-bi ("place of the snow peaks") and believe that their kachina spirits live among the summits for part of every year before returning to the Hopi mesas in the form of nourishing rain clouds. The ever-shifting play of light over the peaks makes it easy to see why all the region's native tribes revere them. The 1930s Works Progress Administration (WPA) guide to Arizona notes, "At sunrise they appeal gold; at noon they are Carrara marble against a turquoise sky; at sunset they are polished copper, ruby, coral, and finally amethyst."

The tallest is **Humphreys Peak,** Arizona's highest point at 12,633 feet, home to a ski resort and miles of hiking trails. The views there are fabulous, from flower-splashed meadows all the way down to the Painted Desert and—if it's a clear day—the Grand Canyon. The 18,960-acre **Kachina Peaks Wilderness** encloses the highest slopes of the San Francisco Peaks, which were formed during the mountain's most recent eruption, about two million years ago. At their center is a huge caldera, the Inner Basin, filled with aspens, pines, and firs.

The easiest way to explore the peaks is via the paved road to the **Arizona Snowbowl,** which leaves Highway 180 seven miles north of downtown and climbs another seven to the ski resort. In the winter, 32 runs are served by four lifts. During summer months, the **Arizona Snowbowl Skyride** (928/779-1951, www.arizonasnowbowl.com, 10 A.M.–4 P.M. Fri.–Sun. and holiday Mon., Memorial Day–mid-Oct., $12 adults, $8 seniors and youth, under seven free) carries visitors to 11,500 feet for panoramic views. At the base of the lift, the Peak Side Café serves snacks and sandwiches for lunch ($10 and under).

Schultz Pass Road (FR 420), a dirt road suitable for passenger cars or bikes, loops 26 miles, passing trailheads and shady meadows where it's easy to while away a couple hours picnicking or watching for elk, wild turkey, and other forest creatures. To get there, drive two miles north of Flagstaff, turning right (east) just after passing the Museum of Northern Arizona. The road ends east of the peaks on U.S. 89, where you can turn right (south) and continue back to Flag. The 2010 Schultz Fire damaged some sections; check with the Flagstaff Ranger District (928/526-0866, www.fs.usda.gov/coconino) for current road conditions.

The **Around the Peaks Loop** is a scenic 44-mile dirt and gravel route that's open April–November, weather permitting. This drive is especially pretty in autumn, when the aspens are turning gold. To do the loop counterclockwise, drive 14 miles north of Flagstaff

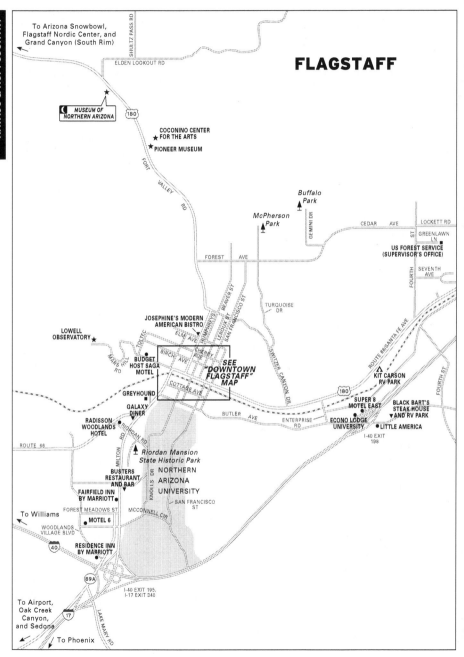

FLAGSTAFF

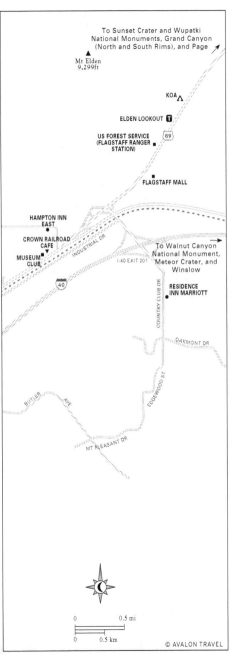

To Sunset Crater and Wupatki
National Monuments, Grand Canyon
(North and South Rims), and Page

Mt Elden
9,299ft

KOA ⋀

ELDEN LOOKOUT ℹ

US FOREST SERVICE
(FLAGSTAFF RANGER
STATION) 89

FLAGSTAFF MALL

HAMPTON INN
EAST

CROWN RAILROAD
CAFE
MUSEUM
CLUB
INDUSTRIAL DR

To Walnut Canyon
National Monument,
Meteor Crater, and
Winslow
I-40 EXIT 201

40

RESIDENCE
INN MARRIOTT

COUNTRY CLUB DR

OAKMONT DR

BUTLER AVE

EDGEWOOD ST

MT PLEASANT DR

0   0.5 mi
0   0.5 km

© AVALON TRAVEL

on U.S. 89 to FR 418, west 12 miles to FR 151 (also known as the Hart Prairie Road), and then south 8 miles to rejoin U.S. 180 about 10 miles north of Flagstaff. The **Nature Conservancy** (928/774-8892, ext. 5, www. nature.org) administers a 245-acre preserve at Hart Prairie, with guided nature walks on Sundays, mid-June–mid-October.

◖ Museum of Northern Arizona

Founded in 1928, this outstanding museum located three miles northwest of downtown Flagstaff (3101 N. Fort Valley Rd., 928/774-5213, www.musnaz.org, 9 A.M.–5 P.M. daily, $7 adults, $4 children) makes an ideal introduction to the human and natural history of the Colorado Plateau. Displays on anthropology, biology, geology, paleontology, and fine art are comprehensive without being exhausting, even though the museum curates more than 600,000 artifacts. The histories of the Colorado Plateau's tribes are a main focus, and exquisite weavings, katsina carvings, baskets, pottery, jewelry, and other crafts are displayed. The museum's Kiva Gallery recreates a kiva with a modern mural by the late Michael Kabotie and Delbridge Honanie, founders of Group Hopid, artists who took tribal traditions in new directions. Changing exhibits examine such topics as the role of Native Americans in Westerns. Programs include monthly behind-the-scenes tours of museum archives, hands-on activities for kids and adults, and guided excursions to locations around the Colorado Plateau. MNA's celebrated summer heritage programs spotlight Zuni, Hopi, Navajo, and Latino traditions, with arts and crafts, dances, storytelling, food, and other activities filling the museum's courtyard and grounds one weekend a month.

Pioneer Museum

The 1908 Coconino County Hospital for the Indigent was converted to a boardinghouse and then a museum in 1963. Today the northern division of the Arizona Historical Society administers the museum (2340 N. Fort Valley Rd., 928/774-6272, http://arizonahistorical-society.org, 9 A.M.–5 P.M. Mon.–Sat., $5 pp

© KATHLEEN BRYANT

The Museum of Northern Arizona is a good introduction to the land and cultures of the Colorado Plateau.

adults, children free). The collection includes more than 10,000 bits of Flagstaff's past, from an old iron lung to farm gear and clothing. Nearby are a 1910 barn, a 1912 steam locomotive, and a historic cabin that was moved there from the east side of the San Francisco Peaks. In summer and fall, the museum hosts walking tours of historic downtown, the annual Wool Festival, and other events featuring reenactors, craft demonstrations, music, and cookouts.

Lowell Observatory

Boston aristocrat-turned-astronomer Percival Lowell founded this observatory (1400 W. Mars Hill Rd., 928/774-3358, www.lowell. edu, 9 A.M.–5 P.M. daily, from noon Nov.–Feb., $10 adults, $4 children) in 1894. He spent 15 years gazing at Mars through the 24-inch refractor telescope, convinced that he was looking at the remains of canals built by an intelligent race. On that matter he was way off, but his hunch about "Planet X" orbiting beyond Uranus proved correct: 14 years after

Lowell's death in 1916, Pluto was discovered by Clyde Tombaugh, and Lowell is given most of the credit. Today the privately owned observatory sits at 7,260 feet in the clear mountain air above Flagstaff, and it is still used for serious research. The observatory offers daily tours and evening programs throughout the year. Highlights include the original telescope inside historic Clark Dome (built of native ponderosa pine in the days before power tools), the spectrograph used to prove that the universe is expanding, and photographic plates with the first images of Pluto. During summer months (June 1–Aug. 31), music and food are available on the patio 6 P.M.–8 P.M. Tuesday–Thursday, and telescope viewing programs begin every evening at 8:30 P.M., weather permitting. Held rain or shine, interactive planetarium presentations begin at 7 P.M.

Riordan Mansion
State Historic Park

Brothers Timothy and Michael Riordan

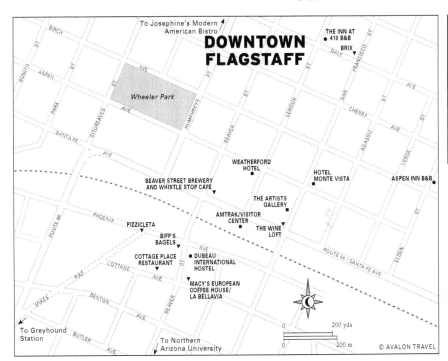

successfully operated the Arizona Lumber and Timber Company near the turn of the 20th century. Each of the two brothers married one of the Metz sisters, cousins of the famous Babbitt Brothers traders. In 1904 they commissioned the architect of the Grand Canyon's El Tovar Hotel to build them a monumental home of logs and volcanic stone, which they called *Kinlichi* (Navajo for "red house"). The Riordan Mansion (409 W. Riordan Rd., 928/779-4395, www.pr.state.az.us, 8:30 A.M.–5 P.M. daily, from 10:30 A.M. Nov.–Apr., $7 adults, $3 children) is actually two separate homes joined by a large rec room—13,000 square feet in all. Michael's side of the 40-room duplex has displays on Flagstaff's lumber industry, and Timothy's side is open for tours. Original fixtures and hand-carved American Craftsman–style furniture give a taste of life at the high end in early Flagstaff. Reservations are a good idea for the guided tours, held hourly, beginning at 9 A.M. in the summer and 11 A.M. in winter. Brown

bag lunches and evening slide presentations, offered on a monthly basis, explore such topics as stagecoach lines or Flagstaff's volcanic past.

The Arboretum at Flagstaff

More than 2,500 species of plants from across the Colorado Plateau thrive at the country's highest research botanical garden (4001 S. Woody Mountain Rd., 928/774-1442, www. thearb.org, 9 A.M.–5 P.M. daily Apr.–Oct., $7 adults, $3 children). The arboretum's 7,150-foot elevation gives it a brief 75-day growing season, yet some 2,500 species are successfully cultivated there, half of which are native to the Four Corners. The collection includes the largest herb garden in the Southwest. Wildflowers are particularly impressive during the summer monsoon season—the best time to visit. Several miles of trails wind through the garden's 200 acres, and guided tours are given daily at 11 A.M., 1 P.M., and 3 P.M. Other activities include weekly bird walks, occasional summer wildflower walks, concerts, classes and workshops, and educational programs for kids.

Elden Pueblo

About 900 years ago, a group of Ancestral Puebloans referred to by archaeologists as the Sinagua (see-NAH-wa) Indians constructed this village situated below Mt. Elden, a lava dome. Their descendants, the Hopis, call the 60- to 70-room pueblo Pasiovi. Since 1978 the Forest Service has administered Elden Pueblo as a public archaeology project to educate visitors. You can tour the ruins (one mile north of the Flagstaff Mall along U.S. 89) year-round, weather permitting. In summer and fall, the Elden Pueblo Project hosts an archaeological field school there. Occasional public dig days are offered. For more information about classes and special events, contact the Elden Pueblo Program Manager at the Coconino National Forest Supervisor's office (928/527-3452).

Sunset Crater Volcano National Monument

The youngest of more than 600 extinct volcanoes in the San Francisco Volcanic Field, Sunset Crater is a cinder cone, 1,000 feet high and nearly a mile wide at its base. Its name comes from the multicolored mineral deposits on the crater rim, which appear to glow with inner fire at sunset. Between A.D. 1040 and 1100, Sunset Crater began to erupt. Flowing lava and forest fires lighted the night sky, and spewing ash traveled 800 square miles. Cinders piled up around the vent, and molten rock oozed through cracks in the earth, transforming the landscape into a stark expanse of cinder drifts and lava hardened into chunks and rough swirls.

A 36-mile **loop road** off U.S. 89 north of Flagstaff connects Sunset Crater (8,029 feet), the Strawberry Crater Wilderness (in the Coconino National Forest), and Wupatki National Monument. It's a fascinating drive through an altered landscape that is slowly transforming once more. Pines, sagebrush, and wildflowers—bursts of bright pink and yellow among the black- and rust-colored cinders—have re-colonized the scorched habitat.

Sunset Crater is on the southern end of the loop. To begin there, turn right 12 miles north of Flagstaff and go two more miles to the newly renovated **visitor center** (928/526-0502, www.nps.gov/sucr, 8 A.M.–5 P.M. daily May–Oct., 9 A.M.–5 P.M. Nov.–Apr., $5), where you'll find displays on volcanism, including a seismograph, as well as a bookstore, picnic tables, and information on daily guided walks and evening programs. Across the road is the U.S. Forest Service's **Bonito Campground** (928/526-0866, mid-May–mid-Oct., $18 per vehicle).

The steep **Lenox Crater Trail** begins a mile east of the visitor center, climbing 0.5 mile to the top of a cinder cone. The elevation and deep cinders will have all but the fittest gasping for breath by the time they reach the top, which offers views of the San Francisco Peaks and surrounding volcanic features. Another half a mile down the park road is the beginning of the **Lava Flow Trail,** a mile-long loop past jagged lava flows, spatter cones, lava tubes, and cinder drifts that look like black snow. A quarter-mile portion of the trail is paved and accessible to wheelchairs.

The entrance fee is good for a week at all three Flagstaff area monuments—Sunset Crater, Wupatki, and Walnut Canyon. A **local passport** ($25) is good for one vehicle for a year.

Wupatki National Monument

Human presence in the Wupatki Basin stretches back 10,000 years. During the 12th century A.D., Ancestral Puebloan clans built several multistory pueblos there after the eruption of nearby Sunset Crater. Prehistoric farmers found growing conditions improved by the water-retaining layer of ash and cinders, using it as a mulch to make up for the area's dry location in the rain shadow of the San Francisco Peaks. (About seven inches of precipitation fall there every year.) Wupatki Pueblo became the largest in the area, home to perhaps 100 people, with several thousand more living nearby in smaller villages. It was a hub of different cultures and influences, evidenced by the adjacent Mesoamerican-style ball court and artifacts that included parrot feathers, copper bells, and shell jewelry. By the mid-13th century, however, most clans moved on to the north, east, and south, where they were assimilated into other villages and cultures.

The **visitor center** (928/679-2365, www.nps.gov/wupa, 9 A.M.–5 P.M. daily, $5 adults) has a picnic area, vending machines, and a bookstore. Interpretive exhibits explain how people subsisted in the Wupatki Basin and surrounding areas and provide an excellent overview of cultural relationships in the Southwest. Ask about orientation programs and guided hikes, held occasionally in summer and more often in spring and fall.

A short self-guided trail leads to the multistory **Wupatki Pueblo,** constructed from reddish Moenkopi sandstone and chunks of volcanic basalt. The trail circles the 100-room pueblo, passing rooms once used to house rangers. The nearby ball court is the northernmost one yet found. The trail to the ball court passes a blowhole, a small opening that expels or draws in air depending on barometric pressure, one of many fascinating geological features found inside the monument.

A side branch from the loop road leads 2.5 miles to **Wukoki,** which may have housed two or three families and is arguably the monument's most striking pueblo, rising high atop a stone outcropping. The loop road leads northwest to several other pueblos. The 30-room **Citadel** stands like a castle on a small butte above **Nalakihu,** which is about half as big. **Box Canyon Pueblo** is perched on either rim of a small canyon en route to pretty **Lomaki.** All these ancient villages share views of the San Francisco Peaks, which continue to be revered by contemporary Indian cultures.

Walnut Canyon National Monument

This deep, lush canyon eight miles east of Flagstaff was home to at least 100 members of the Sinagua culture in the 12th and 13th centuries. Villagers built masonry dwellings in shallow alcoves on the canyon's steep walls and raised corn, beans, and squash in fields among the pine forests at its rim. Limestone ledges are embedded with marine fossils, and

the sandstone gorge continues to shelter abundant vegetation and wildlife. Eventually the Sinaguas moved on; today some Hopi clans trace their ancestry to Walnut Canyon.

Six miles of the 20-mile canyon are protected today, including more than 300 masonry ruins. The **visitor center** (928/526-3367, www.nps.gov/waca, 8 A.M.–5 P.M. May–Oct., 9 A.M.–5 P.M. Nov.–Apr., $5 adults) sits on the edge of the 400-foot-deep canyon, with exhibits on the Sinagua culture and a bookstore. Ranger-guided hikes are held in summer. Allow an hour for the self-guided, paved **Island Trail** (one mile round-trip), which climbs down into the canyon past the ruins of 25 cliff dwellings. The trail's steepness and the altitude (6,700 feet) make it harder than you'd think. The shorter, easier Rim Trail leads past canyon overlooks, a pit house, and a small pueblo.

Watch for the canyon's varied wildlife, which inhabits several overlapping ecological communities. About 70 species of mammals in the area include coyotes, mule deer, elk, mountain lions, black bears, pronghorn antelopes, and a host of smaller critters. Most species are crepuscular (active at dawn and dusk), but you'll see and hear some of the 121 resident bird species, such as canyon wrens, Cooper's hawks, turkey vultures, and white-throated swifts.

To get there, take I-40 east to exit 204 and drive south three miles to the visitors center.

ENTERTAINMENT AND EVENTS

Thanks to its large student population and its role as Northern Arizona's major city, Flagstaff is a shopping hub and entertainment center, with dozens of venues, from concert halls to pool halls. For the latest word on events, as well as restaurant reviews, movie schedules, and current entertainment listings, pick up a copy of *Flagstaff Live!,* the free local weekly that hits the streets Thursday mornings.

Nightlife

Built in 1931, **The Museum Club** (3404 E. Rte. 66, 928/526-9434) has evolved into one of the best country-music roadhouses in the United States. Enter through the split-pine archway

VISITING ANCIENT SITES

The Four Corners region is in many ways an outdoor museum, and the dry, rocky environment has preserved a vast collection of artifacts and dwellings over hundreds, even thousands, of years. With increased visitation, these fragile resources are showing wear, and land managers are often faced with the dilemma of limiting access to preserve scientific and historic values versus encouraging public appreciation and enjoyment. There's something magical about looking up from a hike to spot a Sinaguan granary tucked into a shadowy alcove, or coming across a finely crafted obsidian point and imagine its maker. To help preserve that sense of discovery for those who travel after you, practice the following ethics:

- Don't stand, sit, or climb on walls. Supervise your children. It only takes a moment to destroy something that has stood for centuries (and you wouldn't want to become part of a site for future archaeologists to uncover).

- Don't remove artifacts or pile them up like booty. Context is part of the archaeological record, and once a potsherd or stone flake is moved, that clue to the past is missing.

- Don't camp or burn anything in sites, including cigarettes, incense, or candles.

- Don't eat your lunch in a ruin. Crumbs attract rodents, and rodent activity can undermine walls or damage artifacts.

- Don't allow pets to dig, urinate, or defecate in sites.

- Don't deface rock art. This includes touching. You may think your hands are squeaky-clean, but your skin has oils that can damage the patina and impact future scientific study.

Archaeology is an evolving science, and new research methods are being developed all the time. Activities we don't think twice about today may impact future research. An oft-repeated tale focuses on a pioneer archaeologist who burned roof beams in his campfires, blithely unaware that a nifty new technique for dating ruins would develop from dendrochronology (tree-ring dating).

All archaeological sites on public land and Indian lands are protected by the Archaeological Resources Protection Act (1979) and other laws. Violation can result in felony prosecution, with imprisonment, impoundment, and very stiff fines. If you see someone vandalizing a site, contact the land manager (park service, national forest, or BLM) as soon as possible.

onto the state's largest wooden dance floor. Five more ponderosas support the A-frame roof, and the mahogany bar in the back dates to the 1880s. For more live music, you can head downtown to **Mia's Lounge** (26 S. San Francisco, 928/774-3315), **Altitudes** (2 S. Beaver, 928/214-8218), or the **Green Room** (15 N. Agassiz, 928/226-8669), a few of the establishments popular with the college crowd. There you'll also find several brewpubs within walking distance, including **Flagstaff Brewing** (16 E. Rte. 66, 928/773-1442).

The Arts

NAU's College of Arts and Letters (928/523-8632, www.nau.edu/cal) holds a variety of exhibits, performances, and events at various venues around campus. The **Richard E. Beasley Gallery** (928/523-4612, 10 A.M.–5 P.M. Tues., Thurs., Fri.) displays rotating exhibits of contemporary art by students and faculty on the second floor of the School of Art. Eighteenth-century furniture, glassware, silver, and art fill the **Marguerite Hettel Weiss Collection** on the third floor of the Old Main building. These galleries are both under the auspices of the **Old Main Art Gallery and Museum** (928/523-3471, www.nau.edu/artgallery, noon–5 P.M. Tues.–Sat) on the northern end of campus. Old Main's varied collection is open to the public.

The **Flagstaff Symphony Orchestra** (928/774-5107, www.flagstaffsymphony.org) has been entertaining northern Arizona audiences since 1949. Performances are held in NAU's Ardrey Auditorium September–April, and tickets are available online.

The stately redbrick **Orpheum Theater** (15 W. Aspen St., 928/556-1580, http://orpheumpresents.com) drew movie audiences for decades. Renovated and reenvisioned, the Orpheum now hosts film, concerts, and special events. **Theatrikos** (11 W. Cherry Ave., 928/774-1662, www.theatrikos.com), a community theater company, stages five productions yearly at its historic downtown theater (once home of the Flagstaff Library) and offers outreach programs for kids and adults interested in the dramatic arts. **Coconino Center for the Arts** (2300 N. Fort Valley Rd., 928/779-2300, www.culturalpartners. com, 11 A.M.–5 P.M. Tues.–Sat.), managed by Flagstaff Cultural Partners, hosts a diverse mix of exhibits, film, concerts, art markets, fundraisers, and other events sponsored by local arts organizations.

Events

Every month, dozens of downtown businesses and galleries serve up art, entertainment, and refreshments during Flagstaff's hugely popular **First Friday ArtWalk.** Officially, this street party lasts 6–9 P.M., though many venues continue the celebration into the wee hours.

Annual events begin on New Year's Eve with Flagstaff's very own Pinecone Drop, when crowds huddle in the crisp mountain air to watch as a giant lighted pinecone is lowered from the third-story veranda of the historic Weatherford Hotel. You could say it's both the first and last event of the year because the pinecone drops twice, at 10 P.M. (midnight New York time) to accommodate families and again at midnight Arizona time. In February, Flagstaff's **Winterfest** rolls together more than 100 events, including skiing and sled-dog competitions, sleigh rides, and themed dinners.

Flagstaff may be a winter wonderland, but spring brings a slew of outdoor events. May marks the beginning of the Museum of Northern Arizona's **Heritage Program,** highlighting the food, music, dance, arts, and

traditions of the Colorado Plateau's diverse cultures. The **Hopi Festival** is scheduled around the Fourth of July weekend, with Navajo, Zuni, and Latino festivals held in the months preceding and following.

June weekends are chock-full of activities, from the **Pine Country Pro Rodeo** to the **Flagstaff Folk Festival,** many taking place under shady pines or glittering stars. Fourth of July festivities include a summer pops concert, art fair, and a parade (but not fireworks, when the surrounding forests are tinder-dry). On Labor Day weekend the **Coconino County Fair** takes over 413-acre Fort Tuthill County Park with livestock competitions, exhibits, rides, food, and music. The **Route 66 Festival** rumbles into town mid-September, and the **Flagstaff Festival of Science** (www.scifest. org) stretches into October, when the peaks' aspen groves turn gold.

SHOPPING

It makes sense that Flagstaff—surrounded by mountains, deserts, canyons, and forests—has plenty of good sporting-goods stores. Within a few short blocks downtown, you'll find **Aspen Sports** (15 N. San Francisco St., 928/779-1935), **Babbitt's Backcountry Outfitters** (12 E. Aspen Ave., 928/774-4775), **Mountain Sports** (24 N. San Francisco St., 928/226-2885), and **Peace Surplus** (14 W. Rte. 66, 928/779-4521).

You'll also find stunning landscape photography and Native American arts and crafts. **The Artists Gallery** (17 N. San Francisco St., 928/773-0958) is a cooperative of more than 30 local contemporary artists whose works range from blown glass and paintings to sculpture and furniture. Just down the street, the **Artists Coalition of Flagstaff** (13 N. San Francisco St., 928/522-6969) displays members' works. **Winter Sun Trading Company** (107 N. San Francisco St., 928/774-2884) sells jewelry, old-style kachina dolls, and baskets in the front of the shop. If you'd like to learn more about ethnobotany, head to the back room, where you can buy traditional Hopi herbs or sample one of the sumptuous skincare products formulated

© KATHLEEN BRYANT

Flagstaff's historic downtown has numerous shopping and dining options.

by the owner's daughters. For more Native American crafts, try **Puchteca Indian Crafts** (20 N. San Francisco St., 928/774-2414).

RECREATION
Hiking

From mild strolls to strenuous hikes, Flagstaff boasts some of the best trails in Arizona this close to a city. The 50-mile **Flagstaff Urban Trails System** (FUTS) connects open space to neighborhoods and businesses, and is used by bicyclists, hikers, and runners.

Several trails within the **Mount Elden/Dry Lake Hills Trail System** start from the **Mount Elden trailhead,** near the National Forest Service's **Flagstaff Ranger Station** (5075 N. Hwy. 89, 928/526-0866, 8 A.M.–4:30 P.M. Mon.–Fri.). To get there, take Route 66 east until it becomes U.S. 89, and look across from the Flagstaff Mall. The trails climb up through boulders and huge junipers and piñon pines. **Fatman's Loop** (two miles round-trip, easy) overlooks the city and is named as a warning: A narrow gap between rock formations filters out those who aren't fit. A connecting steep, three-mile trail (one-way) climbs 2,400 feet and leads to the **Elden Lookout Tower** at 9,300 feet, with views as good as you'd expect.

The city's **Buffalo Park** has miles of biking and hiking trails, and serves as a trailhead for the **Oldham Trail** (11 miles round-trip, moderate), climbing through aspen, spruce, pines, and firs to views stretching as far as Oak Creek Canyon, Sunset Crater, and the Painted Desert. To get to Buffalo Park, take San Francisco Street north, turn right on Forest Avenue, which becomes Cedar, and then left on Gemini.

North of town off U.S. 180, the road to **Arizona Snowbowl** offers access to a number of trails, including the popular **Kachina Trail** (10 miles round-trip, moderate) which skirts the San Francisco Peaks, and the challenging **Humphreys Peak Trail** (nine miles round-trip) leading to the highest point in Arizona. (Note that hiking is not allowed off trails above 11,400 feet to protect the fragile tundra vegetation.)

The **Weatherford Trail** (8.7 miles one-way)

© KATHLEEN BRYANT

The Kachina Trail leads through mountainside forest and meadows.

follows a historic roadbed and is popular with families for its moderate climb and good views. This trail, accessible from Schultz Pass Road (FR 420), crosses the Fremont Saddle (11,354 feet) before connecting with the Humphreys Peak Trail from the Arizona Snowbowl. Schultz Pass Road (Apr.–Nov., weather permitting) leaves U.S. 180 just north of the Museum of Northern Arizona. The trailhead is at Schultz Tank, about six miles up the dirt road, which is accessible for most passenger cars.

Northeast of Flagstaff, the trail to the fire tower on top of 8,965-foot **O'Leary Peak** (10 miles round-trip, strenuous) offers excellent views of the Painted Desert, the Inner Basin of the San Francisco Peaks, and nearby Sunset Crater. Like Mount Elden, O'Leary Peak is a lava dome, formed when thick magma oozed up through the earth's crust. To get there, take U.S. 89 north 12 miles, turning right (east) at the road to Sunset Crater Volcano National Monument. Turn left on paved FR 545A just before the campground and visitors center. The

trail begins at the parking area, about a quarter mile down the road.

An easier climb with good views is to the top of 5,589-foot **Doney Mountain,** a cinder cone located on forest land at the edge of Wupatki National Monument. To get to the trail (1 mile round-trip, easy), drive 22 miles north of Flagstaff and turn right (east) at the road to Wupatki. Drive another 9.5 miles to the Doney picnic area and trailhead. Interpretive signs tell about prospector Ben Doney and the two prehistoric ruins that lie along the trail. At the top, you can see the Hopi Buttes—dark volcanic cores that rise above the desert 40 miles away. (The buttes serve as horizon markers for the Hopis' ceremonial calendar.)

For detailed information on these and many other trails, pick up a local hiking guide at one of Flagstaff's numerous outfitter stores.

Biking

Road bikes can get you around town on the **Flagstaff Urban Trails System** (FUTS), which has 50-plus miles of trails and another

80 miles in the works. About half of the existing trail miles are paved, and the rest are hard-packed aggregate. Trail maps are available at city offices and in shops around town.

Mountain bikers can tackle the 19.6-mile **Mount Elden Loop,** which circles the San Francisco Peaks clockwise by connecting the Schultz Creek, Little Elden, Pipeline, Oldham, and Rocky Ridge Trails. This is a popular all-day ride, and most of it is moderately difficult single-track. The trailhead is 3.2 miles north of town on U.S. 180; at milepost 218, turn right and proceed to the intersection of Schultz Pass Road (FR 420) and the Mount Elden Lookout Road (FR 557), where you can park. Head north on the Schultz Creek Trail to begin the loop. **Mount Elden Lookout Road** (FR 557) makes another good ride, one of many in the national forests near town—just be sure to stay out of the wilderness area, where bikes aren't permitted.

Absolute Bikes (202 E. Rte. 66, 928/779-5969, www.absolutebikes.net) sells and rents full-suspension mountain bikes and in-town cruisers; they host group rides several times a week. **Single Track Bikes** (575 W. Riordan Rd., 928/773-1862) is another good source of local riding info, gear, and service.

Winter Activities

The **Arizona Snowbowl** (928/779-1951, 9 A.M.–4 P.M. daily Dec.–mid-Apr., depending on snow conditions) hosts a ski school and has 32 runs for downhill skiers and snowboarders. Lift tickets ($25–50 for adults) provide full- or half-day access to the slopes. Two lift-side lodges have snack bars and rental shops, with overnight lodges and cabins at the base of the mountain.

For cross-country skiing and snowshoeing, head for the **Flagstaff Nordic Center** (928/220-0550, www.flagstaffnordiccenter.com, 9 A.M.–4:30 P.M. daily mid-Dec.–Mar., depending on snow conditions, $8–18 pp) for miles of groomed trails, plus full moon tours, skiing clinics, and equipment rentals. The Nordic Center is 16 miles north of Flagstaff off U.S. 180 at mile marker 232. Other cross-country skiing trails and a snow-play area can be found on Wing Mountain (602/923-3555,

9 A.M.–4 P.M. daily, depending on snow conditions, $12 per vehicle), eight miles northwest of Flagstaff via U.S. 180 and FR 222B.

Guided Tours

In addition to being a popular home base for Grand Canyon river trips, Flagstaff is the starting point for a variety of adventures near and far. **Four Season Outfitters & Guides** (1051 S. Milton Rd., 928/525-1552 or 877/272-5032, www.fsguides.com) organizes hiking, backpacking, climbing, and kayaking tours throughout the Four Corners. Day hikes into the Grand Canyon are $179, including transport, food, and park admission, and can be lengthened up to a week and more. Four days in the Escalante canyons are $985 per person. They have a retail shop on the premises where you can buy or rent gear.

The Museum of Northern Arizona's **Ventures** programs (928/774-5211, ext. 230, www.mnaventures.org, ventures@musnaz.org) explore the Colorado Plateau's canyons and Indian reservations. Offerings range from day trips around Flagstaff's volcano country to wilderness trips in the Grand Canyon or the Escalante. MNA will also put together custom trips for groups. Trip leaders include professional geologists and archaeologists, and prices range $350–1,600, with hotel-based trips on the higher end.

Hitchin' Post Stables (928/774-1719) leads trail rides ($85–150) into Walnut Canyon, southeast of Flagstaff. Riders might spot wildlife like elk or porcupines, or view prehistoric Indian ruins tucked into cliff alcoves.

The **Nature Conservancy** (928/774-8892, ext. 5, www.nature.org) leads 90-minute nature walks focusing on the flora and fauna of Hart Prairie. The free tours depart from the Fort Valley Shopping Center at 10 A.M. each Sunday morning, mid-June–mid-October.

ACCOMMODATIONS

As northern Arizona's main tourist center, Flagstaff has an abundance of lodging options, from primitive camping to resorts. Rates fall by as much as half in the off-season.

Under $50

Between downtown and NAU, two highly re-garded hostels operate under single manage-ment, **Grand Canyon International Hostel** (19½ S. San Francisco, 928/779-9421 or 888/442-2696, www.grandcanyonhostel.com), open year-round, and **Dubeau International Hostel** (19 W. Phoenix, 928/774-6731 or 800/398-7112), closed in winter. Both offer dorm-style rooms ($18–20) or private doubles ($44–48). Breakfast is included, and it's a good idea to book private rooms a few weeks or even a month in advance, especially in the summer. They organize trips to Sedona ($60 pp) and the Grand Canyon ($85 pp) several days a week, and offer Internet access, a cable TV/VCR room, and laundry services.

Many inexpensive motels (some with great old neon signs) line Route 66 on its way out of town. The **Budget Host Saga Motel** (820 W. Rte. 66, 928/779-3631, www.budgethost.com) has rooms for under $50.

$50-100

On January 1, 1900, John W. Weatherford opened a hotel in the dusty frontier town of Flagstaff, and it still bears his name. The **◖ Weatherford Hotel** (23 N. Leroux St., 928/779-1919, www.weatherfordhotel.com, $90–140) has gone through various incarna-tions since then—billiard hall, theater, and radio station to name a few—but after two de-cades of work it has been restored to its glory days. Zane Grey penned *The Call of the Canyon* while staying there. Period touches include a 19-foot lobby ceiling, the wraparound third-floor balcony, and a huge wooden bar in the ballroom, built for a Tombstone saloon over a century ago. (They have rooms with shared bath for $50–80.) Downstairs, **Charly's** serves breakfast, lunch, and dinner ($5–25) and hosts live music several evenings each week.

The **◖ Hotel Monte Vista** (100 N. San Francisco St., 928/779-6971 or 800/545-3068, www.hotelmontevista.com, $65–125) is Flagstaff's other historical (and, purportedly, haunted) lodge downtown. Since it was built in 1927, it has hosted presidents and Hollywood

stars, including John Wayne, who reported a friendly ghost in his room. Most of the 50 rooms on its four floors have good views, and all are named after famous guests. Downstairs, the **Rendezvous** is a coffeehouse by day and martini bar by night, and the cool **Monte Vista Lounge** has billiard tables and live bands on weekends.

A number of chain hotels also fall into this price category, including the **Motel 6** (2475 S. Woodlands Village Blvd., 928/779-3757) and the **Super 8 Motel East** (3725 Kasper Ave., 928/526-0818).

$100-150

You'll also find a number of chain hotels in this range. Try the **EconoLodge University** (914 S. Milton Rd., 928/774-7326) or the **Fairfield Inn by Marriott** (2005 S. Milton Rd., 928/773-1300 or 800/574-6395). Other choices include Best Western, Hampton Inn, Hilton, Holiday Inn, Howard Johnson, La Quinta, and Quality Inn. Several are located near the south end of Milton Rd., with quick access to I-17 and I-40 and numerous nearby stores and restaurants.

Over $150

C. B. Wilson, cousin to Wyatt Earp, built the graceful 1912 home three blocks from down-town that has been turned into the **Aspen Inn Bed & Breakfast** (218 N. Elden St., 928/773-0295 or 888/999-4110, www.flagstaffbed-breakfast.com, $130–170). The owners speak German, Spanish, Italian . . . and English.

Some of the nine rooms at **◖ The Inn at 410 Bed & Breakfast** (410 N. Leroux St., 928/774-0088 or 800/774-2008, www.inn410.com, $150–200) have fireplaces and/or whirlpool tubs. The owners of the 1894 Craftsman home, which was at one time the home of NAU's Sigma Nu fraternity, offer gourmet breakfasts and can arrange packages that include a tour of the Grand Canyon. They've repeatedly won awards as one of the best bed-and-breakfasts in the state.

Situated on 500 acres of ponderosa pines, **Little America** (2515 E. Butler Ave., 928/779-7900 or 800/865-1401, www.littleamer-ica.com/flagstaff, $140–200) has 247 units decorated with imported marble, a heated outdoor pool, and a restaurant. For suites with kitchens, head to the north edge of town and the **Residence Inn by Marriott** (3440 N. Country Club Dr., 928/526-5555 or 888/236-2427, $140–220). The **Radisson Woodlands Hotel** (1175 W. Rte. 66, 928/773-8888, $160–200) offers a heated outdoor pool, the Sakura Japanese restaurant, and a café.

Campgrounds

Year-round choices include **Black Bart's RV Park** (2760 E. Butler Ave., 928/774-1912), which has 174 wooded tent and RV sites for $26–30 near I-40 exit 198. They also have a saloon and an antiques store, and host a musical revue in the steakhouse. The **Flagstaff KOA** (5803 N. Hwy. 89, 928/526-9926 or 800/562-3524) offers both campsites ($30–50) and cabins ($55), five miles northeast of town near I-40, exit 201.

You can camp just about anywhere in the national forest that surrounds Flagstaff; just make sure you're not on private land (signs, fences, and houses are good clues), and be very careful with fires in this tinderbox woodland. Some forest roads close due to winter conditions; contact the Flagstaff Ranger District (5075 N. Hwy. 89, 928/526-0866, www.fs.usda.gov/coconino, 8 A.M.–4:30 P.M. Mon.–Fri.) for more information. Coconino National Forest manages **Bonito Campground** on the loop road near Sunset Crater Volcano National Monument, with 43 sites open April–October for $18.

FOOD

Flagstaff has an impressive variety of places to eat, with plenty of options—including pizza joints, sandwich shops, and ethnic restaurants—priced for student budgets.

Downtown

Many restaurants are located in the rapidly gentrifying area south of the train tracks on Beaver Street, close to NAU. **La Bellavia** (18 S. Beaver St., 928/774-8301, breakfast and lunch daily, $5–10) is a comfy spot that has earned Flagstaff's "best breakfast" title many times

since they opened in 1976. Try their signature Swedish oat pancakes. The smell of fresh-roasted coffee permeates **Macy's European Coffee House, Bakery and Vegetarian Restaurant** (14 S. Beaver St., 928/774-2243, all meals daily) thanks to the big red roaster by the tables. The creative menu includes soups, salads, and sandwiches for $5–10. A few blocks away **Biff's Bagels** (1 S. Beaver St., 928/226-0424, 7 A.M.–3 P.M. Mon.–Sat., 8 A.M.–2 P.M. Sun.) serves breakfast, coffees, and bagels, with sandwiches in the $5 range. They also have Internet access.

Pizza lovers will have a hard time choosing among the options, but if Neapolitan-style pie is your fave, check out **Pizzicletta** (203 W. Phoenix Ave., 928/774-3242, 5 P.M.–9 P.M. Tues.–Wed., 5 P.M.–10 P.M. Thurs.–Sun., $9–13) and its 900-degree wood-burning oven that turns out crispy, chewy circles of joy. Pizza is also on the menu at the **Beaver Street Brewery and Whistle Stop Café** (11 S. Beaver St., 928/779-0079, lunch and dinner daily, $8 and up), along with bratwurst platters and other casual meals meant to go with their home-brewed ales.

Occupying a restored 1909 bungalow, the 🄲 **Cottage Place Restaurant** (126 W. Cottage Ave., 928/774-8431, dinner Wed.–Sun.) may just be Flagstaff's finest. This intimate spot serves appetizers such as escargots for $7–15 and a wonderful two-person chateaubriand for $75 (à la carte entrées are $20 and up). Their wine list has earned *Wine Spectator* magazine's Award of Excellence six times. Reservations are recommended.

Brix (413 N. San Francisco St., 928/213-1021, dinner daily) is a "farm-focused" restaurant and wine bar in a turn-of-the-century brick carriage house downtown. The menu changes seasonally, with entrées like lamb ragout or pan-roasted scallops ($23–35). There's a well-chosen wine list and wide variety of cheeses to enjoy at the long candlelit bar.

Also downtown is **The Wine Loft** (17 N. San Francisco St., 928/773-9463), serving a light menu daily starting at 3 P.M. (2 P.M. Fri. and Sat.). They offer wines by the glass and Belgian beers, with occasional live music and wine tastings on the first Saturday of each month. **Josephine's Modern American Bistro** (503 N. Humphreys St., 928/779-3400, lunch Mon.–Fri., dinner daily, brunch Sat. and Sun.), housed in a historic *malpais* (volcanic rock) bungalow, serves gourmet lunch sandwiches around $10 and dinner entrées running $20–30. The menu's culinary influences range from Southwestern to Mediterranean and Asian, with such imaginative concoctions as short-rib "pie" topped with sweet potato gnocchi.

Route 66

There's no shortage of restaurants and diners along Route 66, which makes a swing through town from the northeast, but only a handful will give you a sense of traveling back in time to the days of the Mother Road. **Miz Zip's** (2924 E. Rte. 66, 928/526-0104, all meals daily) dishes up down-home meals for less than $10, but be sure to bring cash—credit cards aren't accepted. Meat loaf sandwiches, malts, movie posters, and waitresses in Hawaiian shirts sum up the **Galaxy Diner** (931 W. Rte. 66, 928/774-2466, all meals daily), a neon-and-silver faux Route 66 café that does American road staples for $5 and up. You may feel a bit silly driving through (literally) the **Dog Haus** (1302 E. Rte. 66, 928/774-3211, 6:30 A.M.–10 P.M. Mon.–Sat.), but this popular spot lures 'em in with breakfast burritos, burgers, Polish sausages, and chili dogs for less than $5.

Elsewhere in Town

Busters Restaurant and Bar (1800 S. Milton Rd., 928/774-5155, lunch and dinner daily, $10–25) is an animated place with all-American steaks, seafood, and chicken dishes. Northern Arizona's finest sushi bar is probably **Sakura**, in the Radisson Woodlands Hotel (928/773-9118, lunch Mon.–Sat., dinner daily). They also serve teppanyaki, with entrées starting at $15 for dinner.

If you like music with your prime rib, head to **Black Bart's Steak House and Musical Revue** (2760 E. Butler Ave., 928/779-3142, dinner daily), a Western-themed place where students in NAU's voice program serenade diners over oak-broiled steaks and chicken.

INFORMATION AND SERVICES

The **Flagstaff Convention and Visitors Bureau** (928/774-9541 or 800/842-7293, www.flagstaffarizona.org) runs a **visitors center** in the old train station at 1 East Rte. 66 (8 A.M.–5 P.M. Mon.–Sat., 9 A.M.–4 P.M. Sun.). Stop by the **Flagstaff Ranger District** offices (5075 N. Hwy. 89, 928/526-0866, www.fs.usda.gov/coconino, 8 A.M.–4:30 P.M. Mon.–Fri.) for information about recreation on the Coconino National Forest or to buy maps, passes, or permits. You can pick up an America the Beautiful interagency pass there. You'll find similar information at the Forest Supervisor's office (1824 S. Thompson St., 928/527-3600, www.fs.usda.gov/coconino, 7:30 A.M.–4:30 P.M. Mon.–Fri).

Flagstaff Medical Center (928/779-3366) is the region's largest hospital, with 24-hour emergency services. **Concentra Clinic** (1100 E. Rte. 66, Ste. 100, 928/773-9695) provides walk-in urgent care.

At the main branch of **Flagstaff Public Library** (300 W. Aspen Ave., 928/779-7670, 10 A.M.–9 P.M. Mon.–Thurs., 10 A.M.–7 P.M. Fri., 10 A.M.–6 P.M. Sat.) visitors can use the Internet up to 30 minutes daily at no charge and purchase additional time.

The main post office (2400 Postal Blvd., 928/527-2440) is on Flagstaff's northeast side. There's also a downtown branch (104 N. Agassiz, 928/779-2371).

GETTING THERE AND AROUND

Flagstaff is located at the intersection of I-40, which travels from Albuquerque to Kingman, and I-17, which leads north from Phoenix and Tucson. From Phoenix, Flagstaff is a two-hour drive up I-17.

The **Mountain Line** bus service (928/779-6624, www.naipta.az.gov) operates five different routes daily every 30–60 minutes. **A Friendly Cab** (928/774-4444, www.afriendlycab.com) and **Sun Taxi & Tours** (928/779-1111) offer in-town taxi services as well as service to Phoenix and the Grand Canyon's South Rim.

Open Road Tours (602/997-6474 or 855/563-8830, www.openroadtours.com) offers sightseeing tours from Flagstaff, Phoenix Sky Harbor International Airport, and other locations to Grand Canyon, Sedona, and Indian Country. **Arizona Shuttle** (928/226-8060, ext. 1303, or 800/888-2749, www.arizonashuttle. com) has daily shuttle service from Flagstaff to Sedona, Williams, and the Grand Canyon, with runs several times daily to Phoenix Sky Harbor International Airport.

Greyhound (399 S. Malpais Ln., 928/774-4573) takes advantage of the city's location on I-40 with service to major cities to the east and west. **Amtrak**'s (928/774-8679 or 800/872-7245) Southwest Chief stops at the Flagstaff depot (1 E. Rte. 66, 4:15 A.M.– 11:45 P.M. daily), arriving from Los Angeles or Albuquerque. **US Airways** (800/235-9292, www.usairways.com) flies daily between Phoenix and Pulliam Airport, three miles south of town along I-17. (However, it's usually cheaper to fly to Phoenix and take a bus or shuttle from there.)

Sedona

South of Flagstaff on SR 89A is one of Arizona's most beloved destinations. Equal parts art town, resort retreat, and New Age nexus, Sedona (pop. 10,000) is blessed with unearthly red-rock scenery, a moderate climate at 4,500 feet, and (according to many) a number of "energy vortexes" scattered among the stones. With more massage therapists, yoga teachers, spirit guides, and artists per capita than any other place in the West—not to mention spas and luxury accommodations galore—Sedona makes for a fascinating and wonderfully scenic short trip from Flagstaff.

Getting there is half the fun. SR 89A descends through Oak Creek Canyon for almost half of the 30 miles from Flagstaff to Sedona, a gorgeous drive past rocky cliffs, swimming holes, trailheads, and rustic lodges. The canyon can be very crowded on summer weekends, so consider arriving midweek or during the off-season. The same applies to Sedona itself; it's definitely not off the beaten track, with some four million people making the pilgrimage every year.

History

Some 10,000 years ago, hunter-gatherers wandered red-rock canyons in search of plants and game. After the beginning of the last millennium, people began relying increasingly on agriculture, digging irrigation canals and tanks, outlining garden plots with stone, and employing other strategies for conserving water. The Southern Sinaguas moved from scattered pit houses around A.D. 1100, building stone pueblos inside alcoves, where they lived until congregating in larger hilltop villages during the latter half of the thirteenth century. For a time, these Ancestral Puebloans coexisted with seminomadic bands who arrived from the south around A.D. 1300. But by A.D. 1450, Sinaguan clans had moved on, though many individuals likely stayed behind, intermarrying with the Yavapais, who were visited in turn by Spanish explorers, Mexican and American trappers, prospectors, and eventually settlers and soldiers. The army forcibly removed the Yavapais and Apaches to a reservation in 1875.

Oak Creek Canyon's first Anglo resident was J. J. Thompson, who arrived in 1876 and built a cabin on a site where Indian crops were still growing. He named it Indian Gardens. More families arrived and settled farther down the creek, digging irrigation ditches to water crops and raise orchards. The remote farming community was named in 1902 after the wife of settler T. C. Schnebly, who established the town's first post office. He chose the name Sedona partly because it was short enough to fit on a cancellation stamp.

Author Zane Grey helped popularize the landscape with his novel *The Call of the Canyon,* and Hollywood arrived in the 1940s and 1950s, filming dozens of Westerns, including *Angel*

© KATHLEEN BRYANT

Sedona's red rocks bear names like Coffee Pot, Ship Rock, and Steamboat.

and the Badman (1949) and *Broken Arrow* (1950). In the ensuing decades a new cadre of visitors was drawn by the town's stunning location. Artists, tourists, and retirees came for the scenery and stayed for a variety of reasons, and Sedona gradually became one of the top destinations in the Southwest. The New Age movement of the 1980s brought an influx of seekers. The city was incorporated in 1988, but half of its 19 square miles belongs to the federal government as Coconino National Forest. High-end tourism has begun to replace the desert-love-in vibe of Sedona's early years, but metaphysical inquiry and alternative therapies continue to prevail, along with outdoor recreation and art.

SIGHTS
◖ Oak Creek Canyon
Colorful stone cliffs and pine forests above lush riparian habitat make Oak Creek Canyon one of the most inviting spots in this dry state, drawing hikers, anglers, and swimmers, especially on summer weekends. The canyon mixes public and private land, and SR 89A travels its length from Uptown Sedona to the rim at the top of a series of switchbacks. Three Forest Service campgrounds, numerous picnic areas, and several trailheads are located along the canyon's 14-mile length, along with rustic lodges, residences, and a few shops and restaurants. You can take a dip in Oak Creek at **Grasshopper Point** or at **Slide Rock State Park** (928/282-3034, 8 A.M.–7 P.M. daily in summer, $20 per vehicle), where you can slide down smooth rocks and hike three short trails (all less than a half mile). The park is 6 miles north of Sedona.

At the top of the canyon, **Oak Creek Vista** (9 A.M.–4:30 P.M. daily, weather permitting) offers a splendid overlook. The Forest Service visitor center located there is open March–October. During summer months, Navajo artisans sell jewelry and other crafts under the shade of the vista's ponderosa pines.

Jordan Historical Park
The Sedona Historical Society operates a

© KATHLEEN BRYANT

Oak Creek Canyon is an oasis of shade and cascading waters.

museum (735 Jordan Rd., 928/282-7038, www.sedonamuseum.org, 11 A.M.–3 P.M. daily, $5) on the site of the home and orchards of Walter and Ruth Jordan. During the 1930s, the Jordans built an irrigation system that developed into Sedona's first commercial water supply. Their apple-packing barn has displays on the town's farming history, and the Jordans' red-rock cabin has exhibits on movie-making, ranching, and forestry.

Chapel of the Holy Cross
Sedona's celebrated Chapel of the Holy Cross (780 Chapel Rd., 928/282-4069, www. chapeloftheholycross.com, 9 A.M.–5 P.M. daily, from 10 A.M. Sun.) soars up from a red sandstone outcropping, supported by the large cross that also serves as its central design feature. This Catholic chapel is open to people of all faiths, who come for the panoramic views as well as for the spiritual energy that seems to emanate from the chapel and its surroundings. To get there, take SR 179 south toward the Village of Oak Creek for three miles; then turn left on Chapel Road.

Prehistoric Ruins and Rock Art
Sedona's red-rock canyons and cliffs provided shelter and food to the prehistoric Sinagua Indians. The finest red-rock cliff dwelling in the area is **Palatki** (928/282-3854, 9 A.M.–3 P.M. daily), occupied 800 years ago. A short trail leads to a series of alcoves holding more than 5,000 pictographs and petroglyphs, with docents and rangers on hand to answer questions. Reservations are strongly recommended. To get there, take SR 89A eight miles west of the Y intersection. Just past mile marker 365, turn right on FR 525, a good dirt road suitable for most passenger cars unless it's been raining or snowing. Continue for five miles to a fork; stay right, continuing on FR 795 to the parking lot. After your tour, you can make a scenic loop back to Sedona by turning left (east) on the Boynton Pass Road (FR 152C), which changes from a rough dirt road to pavement after a couple miles. Continue to a T, where you'll turn right, and then right again at the next T onto Dry Creek Road, which will return you to modern civilization.

If you have a sturdy vehicle, you can venture even farther into the cliffs and canyons to visit **Honanki** (10 A.M.–6 P.M. daily, weather permitting). This village and rock art site tucked below Loy Butte is four miles away from Palatki via FR 525. It's a good idea to check in first with the Forest Service (928/282-4119) or the rangers at Palatki (928/282-3854) for directions and current road conditions, or arrive via a Pink Jeep tour.

The **V-V Heritage Site** (9:30 A.M.–3 P.M. Fri.–Mon.) preserves the densest concentration of petroglyphs (rock art pecked into stone) in the area, including a possible solar calendar. It's a short (0.3 mile) stroll to the site, where docents can tell you more about the Sinagua culture. To get there, take SR 179 south of Sedona toward I-17. Continue under the freeway, where the road becomes FR 618. It's three paved miles to the parking lot.

EVENTS
For several years running, Sedona has been named one of the nation's top small art towns,

and many annual events revolve around music and the visual arts. The fabulous **Sedona International Film Festival** (www.sedonafilm-festival.com) arrives the last week of February with parties, workshops, and more than 100 independent movies.

The event calendar peaks in autumn, when the weather is at its best. One of the first fall festivals is **Jazz on the Rocks** (http://sedonajazz.com) with concerts and master classes. Early in October, the weekend-long **Sedona Arts Festival** hosts more than 150 artists, followed a couple of weeks later by the **Plein Air Festival** (www.sedonapleinairfestival.com), when painters work out-of-doors on sidewalks and trails and by creeks. The latter event is sponsored by **Sedona Art Center** (15 Art Barn Rd., 928/282-3809), a beloved community institution with a gallery and classrooms in Uptown.

Mild winters—think red rocks dusted with snow—are the backdrop for outdoor holiday celebrations like Tlaquepaque's candlelit **Festival of Lights,** held on a single evening in early December, and **Red Rock Fantasy,** which sparkles from late November to New Year's Day.

A handful of restaurants host live music on weekend evenings, and there's often something happening at **Oak Creek Brewing Company** (2050 Yavapai Dr., 928/204-1300). You'll find entertainment listings in *Kudos* (www.kudos-az.com), a free newsweekly published on Wednesdays.

SHOPPING

More than 80 galleries and shops sell everything from red-dirt T-shirts to fine art. A good place to start is **Tlaquepaque** (336 Hwy. 179, 928/282-4838, www.tlaq.com), constructed in the 1970s along Oak Creek to resemble the colonial town outside Guadalajara, Mexico, bearing the same name. Tlaquepaque's sycamore-shaded courtyards and arched walkways are home to more than 30 galleries and shops, as well as four restaurants with outdoor dining.

Many other galleries are concentrated along this pleasant, walkable section of SR 179, such as **Sedona Pottery, Garland Rugs** (specializing

in Navajo weavings), **Hozho,** and the **Hillside Sedona** shops and restaurants. On the first Friday evening of each month, a trolley (free) provides transportation between "gallery row" and Uptown, when participating venues host receptions and offer light refreshments.

If you're interested in learning more about Sedona's spiritual side, the **Center for the New Age** (928/282-2085, www.sedonanewagecenter.com), across SR 179 from Tlaquepaque, operates a bit like a clearing house for various practitioners and services. There you can sign up for a guided vortex tour, get a horoscope chart, find a massage therapist, or have your aura cleansed, and then stop next door at **Crystal Castle** (313 SR 179, 928/282-5910), for a psychic reading on the shady porch. In West Sedona, **Crystal Magic** (2978 W. Hwy. 89A, 928/282-1622) and its sister store **Clothing Magic** (2970 W. Hwy. 89A, 928/203-0053) sell New Age music, metaphysical books, Birkenstocks, and, of course, crystals.

RECREATION

There are a gazillion red rocks and almost as many ways to explore them, from bouncing down a dirt road on a jeep to floating overhead in a hot air balloon. Tour options abound, and scenic views are as easy as stepping out the door. A Red Rock Pass ($5 daily, $15 weekly) is required to park at many national forest trails and viewpoints in the Sedona area. Additional fees are charged for popular recreation areas like Call of the Canyon, Grasshopper Point, and Crescent Moon Ranch. Stop in at a visitors center or contact the **Red Rock Ranger District** (928/282-4119 or 928/203-7500, www.re-drockcountry.org) for more information.

Hiking

More than 300 miles of hiking trails wind through the forest or traverse reddish sandstone buttes and mesas with names like Coffee Pot Rock, Snoopy, and the Cockscomb. If you're curious about Sedona's energy vortexes, the most easily accessed is at the saddle of **Airport Mesa.** To get there, turn left on Airport Road as you enter West Sedona. Look for a parking area on the left about halfway up the mesa. It's a short scramble to the saddle, which offers excellent views of Munds and Lee Mountains to the east.

At **Cathedral Rock,** said to be another vortex, you'll find an invigorating slickrock climb to the spires at the heart of this dramatic formation. Acrophobes should think twice about this moderately difficult hike: Though it's a mere 1.5 miles round-trip, it's steep, with ledges and toeholds in some places. For the trailhead, drive 3.5 miles south on SR 179 from the Y intersection. Turn right at Back O' Beyond Road and continue a half mile to the parking area on the left.

Every bit as inspiring is **Boynton Canyon** northwest of Sedona. To get there, take U.S. 89A through West Sedona, turning right (north) on Dry Creek Road and traveling about three miles to the T intersection. Turn left, taking Boynton Pass Road 1.6 miles to another T. Turn right toward Enchantment Resort. The large trailhead parking area outside the resort entrance, often full on weekends, offers access to three trails, including Boynton Canyon Trail (moderate, five miles round-trip). The entire canyon is said to be diffused with energy, though some people say the vortex is centered on Boynton Spires, reached by the short (less than one mile) Vista Trail. In any case, it's all scenic, and by now you may be thinking it's hard to distinguish between vortex energy and the thrill of being outdoors in such a beautiful place.

To continue your experiment, you could hike a "non-vortex" trail to see if you detect a difference. For **Doe Mountain,** a moderate 3.6-mile round-trip climb up a mesa with 360-degree views, take Boynton Pass Road another 1.2 miles to the trailhead. If you'd like a more challenging hike, head across the road from Doe Mountain to the **Bear Mountain Trail** (five miles round-trip, strenuous). This trail alternates between steep climbs and plateaus, and the scenery changes with each section, making it feel like three or four hikes in one. The summit of 6,506-foot Bear Mountain has views all the way north to Flagstaff's San Francisco Peaks.

For more information on Sedona's superb hiking, pick up a copy of a local trail guide or stop in at a visitors center for maps. Another option is to hire **Sedona Private Guides** (928/204-2201, www.sedonaprivateguides. com), who mix good humor and hospitality on a range of outings, from metaphysical-themed walks to challenging hikes.

Biking

Though bikes are not allowed inside Sedona's three wilderness areas, forest roads and trails offer miles of rides. Friendly local bike shops provide trail information and lead tours. Among them are **Absolute Bikes** (6101 SR 179, Ste. C, 928/284-1242, www.absolute-bikes.net/sedona) and **Bike & Bean** (6020 SR 179, 928/284-0210, www.bike-bean.com), both in the Village of Oak Creek, and **Over the Edge** (1695 W. SR 89A, 928/282-1106, www. otesports.com) in West Sedona. Bikes rent for $40–70 per day.

Single-track enthusiasts like **Cathedral Loop** (11.4 miles round-trip, mixing road and trail) and **Little Horse Trail** (3.2 miles round-trip, technical). Paved **Bell Rock Pathway** (seven miles round-trip) is a better choice for road bikes and families with small children. It travels between the Little Horse parking area (south of the Chapel of the Holy Cross) and Courthouse Butte in the Village of Oak Creek.

Scenic Drives and Tours

A half-dozen jeep tour companies call Sedona home, each with its own flavor and at least one exclusive route. Tours start around $50 at **Red Rock Jeep** (270 N. Hwy. 89A, 928/282-6826 or 800/848-7728, www.redrockjeep.com), whose guides dress in Old West garb. **Pink Jeep** offers several options, including a jeep tour ($72) to **Honanki Pueblo,** a 700-year-old cliff dwelling, or a comfy van excursion ($125) to the Grand Canyon.

All tour companies travel **Schnebly Hill Road,** a scenic but rocky route you can explore on your own if you don't mind wear and tear on your vehicle (and your nerves). A high-clearance 4WD is strongly recommended for this adventure. The road begins at the roundabout at the Oak Creek bridge, about a half mile south of the U.S. 89A/179 intersection. At one mile, the pavement ends at a large parking area with picnic tables and trailheads. From there, Schnebly Hill Road changes to a rock-studded route as it winds its way up to the Mogollon Rim, passing the softly rounded red sandstone buttes known as the Cowpies at about three miles. In winter, the road is often closed just past the Merry-Go-Round, a red sandstone formation circled by blocks of gray limestone that make up the carousel "horses." Beyond the Schnebly Hill Vista, a dirt parking area with great views at about six miles, the road levels out and continues another seven miles toward I-17 through a juniper woodland. Instead of continuing to the freeway, most drivers will want to flex their knuckles (now white from gripping the steering wheel), turn around, and head back to Sedona, taking in the views from the other direction.

For a milder scenic drive with a side trip to **Red Rock Crossing,** head a couple miles west of town on SR 89A and turn left (south) on Upper Red Rock Loop Road. The paved road travels past the high school before winding down toward Oak Creek. En route, several pull-outs provide photo opportunities of **Cathedral Rock.** For a closer look or a splash in the creek, turn left on Chavez Road, cross the bridge, and turn right, following the signs for Red Rock Crossing and Crescent Moon Ranch. The **picnic area** (8 P.M.–8 P.M. daily, Memorial day–Labor day, closing at dusk during the off-season, $9/vehicle) is often crowded, and at sunset, photographers flock there for the money shot, when Cathedral Rock's sandstone cliffs turn bright orange and reflect in the waters of Oak Creek.

For less-crowded creek views (but no swimming), continue on the loop road (which changes to a good dirt road for about two miles) to **Red Rock State Park** (928/282-6907, 8 A.M.–5 P.M. daily, $10/vehicle). There you can hike, picnic, and linger along the creek to watch for blackhawks and other wildlife. Nature hikes and programs are offered daily. Twice a month from April–October, park naturalists lead moonlight walks (reservations required). The loop road rejoins SR 89A in another three miles.

Fishing

Anglers can try their luck in Oak Creek Canyon, where cold springs nurture trout introduced at the fish hatchery upstream. The section from Call of the Canyon picnic area south to Junipine is catch-and-release. At Rainbow Trout Farm (3500 N. Hwy. 89A, 928/282-5799, daily), you keep what you catch, and you can use the grills provided for a creekside picnic. Jim McInnis of **Gon' Fishin'** (928/282-0788), a fount of local wisdom, guides trips to favorite canyon fishing holes. Fishing licenses are available at Bashas' grocery store in West Sedona or on the Arizona Game and Fish Department's website (www.azgfd.gov).

ACCOMMODATIONS

Sedona Schnebly was the first to lodge guests in the town named for her, and her legacy of hospitality extends today from rustic canyon lodges to sprawling resorts. Most offer off-season specials, and if you're willing to submit to a timeshare sales pitch, you can shop around for a bargain package that might include a tour and spa services.

Sedona boasts a number of award-winning B&Bs and small inns. In the Village of Oak Creek, the **Canyon Villa Inn of Sedona** (40 Canyon Circle Dr., 800/453-1166, www.canyonvilla.com, $210–320) offers rooms designed around monumental views of Bell Rock and Courthouse Butte, an outdoor heated pool, and gourmet breakfasts. Another AAA four-diamond option, **Casa Sedona B&B Inn** (55 Hozoni Dr., 800/525-3756, www.casasedona.com, $140–280) is located in West Sedona. **El Portal** (95 Portal Ln., 928/203-9405 or 800/313-0017, www.elportalsedona.com, $260–450) re-creates early 1900s Arts-and-Crafts style a few steps away from sycamore-shaded Oak Creek and Sedona's gallery district.

If your budget permits, you can spring for a casita at **Enchantment Resort** (800/826-4180, www.enchantmentresort.com, $400 and up) nestled between the gorgeous red-and-buff sandstone walls of Boynton Canyon. One of the resort's three dining rooms has a telescope focused on a centuries-old cliff dwelling. Amenities include a kids' camp, tennis courts, and the fabulous Mii amo spa.

Even on a modest budget, you can have stunning views, a pool, and a pretty garden for strolling at **Sky Ranch Lodge** (1105 Airport Rd., 928/282-6400 or 800/708-6400, www. skyranchlodge.com, $90–150), perched atop Airport Mesa. (If you're concerned about noise, don't be: Sedona's airstrip is rarely used after dark, and the hotel sits 500 feet above city traffic.) Guests at **Lo Lo Mai Lodge** (50 Willow Way, 928/282-2835, $55–95) in West Sedona are granted access to its sister property in nearby Page Springs, where you can enjoy a cool dip in Oak Creek or a spring-fed pond. In the Village of Oak Creek, the **Sedona Village Lodge** (105 Bell Rock Plaza, 928/284-3626 or 800/890-0521, $50–90) has both standard rooms and suites with kitchenettes.

At-large camping is restricted to certain areas in the forest's Red Rock Ranger District. Contact Coconino National Forest (928/282-4119, www.fs.usda.gov/coconino or www.redrockcountry.org) for details. The Forest Service operates three seasonal campgrounds in Oak Creek Canyon ($16–18, mid-Mar.–mid-Oct.) Some sites can be reserved (877/444-6777, www.recreation.gov), but most are on a first-come, first-served basis and fill quickly on summer weekends. None have utility hookups, and only Pine Flat and Cave Springs can accommodate small RVs. A better choice for RV travelers is **Rancho Sedona** (135 Bear Wallow Ln., 928/282-7255 or 888/641-4261, http://ranchosedona.com, $40–60), a shady creekside oasis just off Schnebly Hill Road.

FOOD

Sedona's food choices range from simple fare to fine dining, including a handful of ethnic choices, a natural-foods deli, and Uptown's tempting sweet shops. What you won't find there are a slew of ubiquitous chains: Even McDonald's forgoes the usual golden arches in favor of a verdigris M.

The **Mesa Grill at the Sedona Airport** (928/282-2400, all meals daily, $8–27) has good food, but the main draw is the awe-inspiring panorama from atop Airport Mesa. Plane buffs can pick a window seat overlooking the mesa's notoriously tricky runway; the rest can feast on red-rock views from the dining room or patio.

Also in West Sedona, the **Heartline Café** (1610 W. SR 89A, 928/282-0785, dinner daily, $15–30) has earned repeat best-restaurant honors. Breakfast and lunch ($6–12) are served next door at Heartline's **Gourmet Express** (928/282-3365). Both locations have pleasant patios for meals al fresco. A bit farther west is **Cuisine of India** (1910 W. SR 89A, 928/204-2300, lunch and dinner daily), serving a mildly spicy lunch buffet for $8.

The elegant **Rene at Tlaquepaque** (336 Hwy. 179, Ste. 118, 928/282-9225, lunch and dinner daily) has an extensive wine list and continental cuisine. Entrées are $8–13 for lunch, $18–28 for dinner. The Southwestern-themed **Cowboy Club** (241 N. SR 89A, 928/282-4200, lunch and dinner daily, $10–35) is a lively venue that occupies one of Sedona's historic Uptown buildings.

◀ **Elote** (771 SR 179, 928/203-0105, dinner Tues.–Sat., $17–22) is popular with locals and visitors alike. Those who manage to get a table (reservations are taken only for parties of five or more) will be wowed by Chef Smedstad's reinterpretation of Mexican cuisine, such as the chiles rellenos stuffed with vegetable-nut *picadillo* and goat cheese.

If you're feeling weak after navigating Uptown's long gauntlet of shops, a stop at **Sedona Memories Bakery & Café** (321 Jordan Rd., 928/282-0032, $5–10) will fortify you with giant sandwiches and cookies. In the Village of Oak Creek, the **Blue Moon Café** (6101 SR 179, Ste. B, 928/284-1831, all meals daily, $7 and up) is a breakfast-all-day kind of place, with hand-tossed pizzas and Philly cheesesteaks.

INFORMATION AND SERVICES

For more information on Sedona and the surrounding area, contact the **Sedona-Oak Creek Chamber of Commerce** (1 Forest Rd.,

928/282-7722 or 800/288-7336, www.visitsedona.com, 8:30 A.M.–5 P.M. Mon.–Sat., 9 A.M.–3 P.M. Sun.).

The **Red Rock District visitors center** (8375 SR 179, 928/282-4119 or 928/203-7500, www.redrockcountry.org, 8 A.M.–5 P.M. daily) lies south of the Village of Oak Creek along SR 179. Along with informative displays and a retail area with books and maps, it offers a wide veranda with awesome views of Bell Rock, Courthouse Butte, and other formations. The ranger district's northern gateway is at the vista overlook at the top of Oak Creek Canyon, open 9 A.M.–4 P.M. daily, March–October, weather permitting.

The **Sedona Library** (3250 White Bear Rd., 928/282-7714, Mon.–Sat.) has computers for visitors who want to check their email. (Be sure to pause at the library's entrance and admire the statue of Sedona Schnebly made by sculptor Susan Kliewer.)

The main **post office** (928/282-3511) is located at the intersection of SR 89A and SR 179. Sedona Medical Center (3700 W. SR 89A, 928/204-3000 or 928/204-4100) has 24-hour emergency services. Nonemergencies can be handled at Sedona Urgent Care (2530 W. SR 89A, 928/203-4813).

GETTING THERE AND AROUND

Sedona is roughly divided into three areas along SR 89A and SR 179: Uptown, the bustling strip of shops along SR 89A north of its intersection with SR 179; West Sedona, a quieter, mostly residential section west of the intersection; and the Village of Oak Creek, an unincorporated area of residences, resorts, and shops approximately seven miles south of the intersection en route to I-17. If you stop to ask for directions, keep in mind that locals still refer to the 89A/179 intersection as "the Y," even though it has been reconfigured into a double roundabout.

Though less than 30 miles south of Flagstaff,

allow an hour for the winding drive through Oak Creek Canyon on SR 89A to Sedona. Sedona is about two hours north of Phoenix via I-17. You can exit the freeway at SR 260 (exit 289) or SR 179 (exit 311). The former route passes through Cottonwood and joins SR 89A for the Dry Creek Scenic Road. The latter follows the Scenic Red Rock Byway between the Village of Oak Creek and Sedona. Whichever route you choose to get there, the views are great.

Though it's easy to get around in your own vehicle, if you prefer to have someone else introduce you to the sights, the **Sedona Trolley** (276 Hwy. 89A, 928/282-4211, $12) has two routes that give riders a narrated overview of the town's layout and vistas. The **Verde Lynx** (928/282-0938, $2) connects Sedona to the Verde Valley community of Cottonwood, making several in-town stops and running until early evening. Sedona is known to roll up the sidewalks early, but if you're out late, you can call **Bob's Taxi** (928/282-1234) or hire **White Tie Transportation** (928/203-4500) to usher you around in a limo or luxury SUV. (A lot of folks tie the knot in Sedona, so livery options are plentiful for a small town.)

Jeep rental companies like Barlow's (928/282-4344 or 888/928-5337) will provide maps and information about 4WD trails. Barlow's is located next to Hertz (3009 W. SR 89A, 928/282-0878 or 800/654-3131). At the airport terminal, Discount Rent-a-Car (877/467-8578) offers hourly rentals in addition to standard rates.

The **Sedona Airport** (235 Terminal Dr., 928/282-1046, www.sedonaairport.org) hosts five fixed-wing and helicopter tour companies, charter air services, and a restaurant.

The **Sedona-Phoenix Shuttle** (928/282-2066, $50 one-way, $90 round-trip) travels from Sky Harbor Airport in Phoenix to the Village and West Sedona.

Grand Canyon National Park

One of the world's greatest natural wonders awaits a mere 90 minutes northwest of Flagstaff. The Grand Canyon's mile-deep chasm reveals layers of rock laid down over two billion years and then carved out by the relentless force of flowing water. This colorful gash through the high Colorado Plateau is the canyon to end all canyons: 277 miles long and up to 18 miles wide, with countless side gorges, each of which could be a national park in itself.

The Colorado River flows through the canyon's heart, tumbling over 160 rapids and dropping more than 2,000 feet by the time it reaches the Grand Wash Cliffs marking its western edge. The canyon's diverse environments, from riparian to desert to boreal forest, are home to more than 2,000 species. Regional tribes have revered the Grand Canyon for centuries, and yet it was one of the last places in the United States to be mapped. Established in 1919, Grand Canyon National Park (928-638-7888, www.nps.gov/grca, $25 per vehicle for one week) has become one of the country's greatest tourist draws, and justifiably so. The view from the edge is something you'll never forget, and a trip to the bottom—particularly a raft voyage through the famous Colorado River rapids—is almost beyond words.

THE SOUTH RIM

Most visitors approach Grand Canyon National Park from its south side, which offers the quickest access from Flagstaff and Phoenix. As a result, the South Rim has more tourist amenities than the canyon's remote North Rim. From Flagstaff, three routes lead to the South Rim's main tourism center, Grand Canyon Village. The shortest is from downtown Flagstaff via U.S. 180 (78 miles). You can also take I-40 to Williams and then SR 64 to the canyon (80 miles). To enter the park at its less-used East Entrance Station, take U.S. 89A to SR 64. Though this route is twenty miles longer, you'll travel through the Navajo Reservation and along Desert View Drive en route to Grand Canyon Village.

Grand Canyon Village

The heart of the park's largest developed area is historic Grand Canyon Village, where you'll find lodges and buildings dating to the early 1900s, including the train depot, El Tovar Hotel, and several of architect Mary Colter's fabulous creations: Lookout Studio, Hopi House, Hermits Rest, and Bright Angel Lodge. Between the South Rim Entrance Station and the village are a post office, a bank, medical services, and the main visitors center (8 A.M.–5 P.M. daily) at **Canyon View Information Plaza.** The plaza, where you'll also find parking, shops, restrooms, a theater, and informative kiosks, is located across from **Mather Point.**

The **Rim Trail,** accessible from Mather Point and several locations within Grand Canyon Village, offers a pleasant walk to scenic overlooks, where you can get a sense of the vastness of the canyon and its tributaries. The mostly paved trail is 12 miles long, but it can easily be hiked in sections.

Hermits Rest Road

West of Grand Canyon Village, an eight-mile paved road leads to Hermits Rest, a historic building designed by architect Mary Elizabeth Jane Colter, now a visitors center and gift shop. The **Hermit Trail** begins there, the start of a multiday backpacking trip for those with permits, or an invigorating day hike to Santa Maria Spring or Dripping Springs. En route to Hermits Rest are some of the South Rim's most panoramic overlooks, including **Hopi Point, Pima Point,** and the **Abyss,** where the canyon's cliffs plummet a mile deep. The park's free shuttles travel the road March–November. During winter months, the road (also known as West Rim Drive) is open to passenger cars, weather permitting.

© KATHLEEN BRYANT

Mather Point is a popular overlook on Grand Canyon's South Rim.

Desert View Drive

State Route 64 runs east from Grand Canyon Village for 25 miles along the edge of the canyon, where it's called Desert View Drive or East Rim Drive. Along the way are ruins, scenic overlooks, and the **Desert View Watchtower,** a stone structure designed by Mary Colter for the Fred Harvey Company in 1932 and lined with murals that represent different cultural periods. SR 64 continues east to Cameron.

Accommodations and Food

Six national park lodges offer accommodations on the South Rim, including the grand old ◖ **El Tovar,** built in 1905. Rooms range $166–300, depending on the season. For reservations, contact Xanterra Parks & Resorts (303/297-2757 or 888/297-2757, www.grandcanyonlodges.com). Most of the lodges have restaurants. You can camp at **Mather Campground** (877/444-6777, www.recreation.gov, $18 per vehicle, open year-round) and its attached **Trailer Village** ($25 per vehicle) in Grand Canyon Village, or at **Desert View**

Campground (May–Oct., $12 per vehicle, no reservations or hookups), 26 miles east.

More tourist services are available a couple miles south of park boundaries in the town of **Tusayan,** on SR 64.

Getting There and Around

Shuttle companies in Flagstaff make daily runs to Grand Canyon Village and Tusayan. From Williams, you can take the charming **Grand Canyon Railway** (800/843-8724, www.thetrain.com). The 2.5-hour ride is $65–170 per person ($35–100 children), but various packages including tours and lodging are available.

The park's free shuttle-bus system runs between Grand Canyon Village, Mather Point, and the South Kaibab trailhead, extending spring through fall to cover Hermit Road. For those staying in Tusayan, just south of the park's entrance, a commuter shuttle operates during summer months.

◖ THE NORTH RIM

Though only about 10 miles from the South Rim as the raven flies, the less-developed North

Grand Canyon's cooler and quieter North Rim is open from mid-March to mid-October.

Rim is more than 200 miles away by road, so it sees far fewer visitors. You can still depend on stupendous views and precipitous trails—but you'll have several thousand fewer people to share them with. Plus, since it's over 1,000 feet higher, the North Rim is significantly cooler in summer . . . and closes due to heavy snows in the winter.

Bright Angel Point

The North Rim's main developed area is at Bright Angel Point, where you'll find the **North Rim Visitors Center** (8 A.M.–6 P.M. daily May–Oct.), as well as lodging, camping, dining, and shopping options.

Day hikes near the lodge include the paved **Bright Angel Point Trail** (0.5-mile one-way, easy) and the **Transept Trail** (3 miles one-way, easy) from the lodge to the campground. Three longer trails start a couple of miles north of the lodge, including the popular **North Kaibab Trail,** which leads backpackers 14 miles into the canyon, where it connects to trails originating on the South Rim. Day hikers can take the

North Kaibab Trail to the Coconino Overlook (1.5 miles round-trip, moderate) or Roaring Springs (10 miles round-trip, strenuous).

Cape Royal Drive

A paved 23-mile scenic drive leads to **Cape Royal,** passing a half-dozen overlooks along the way, many with picnic areas and short trails. From Cape Royal, you can see all the way across to the South Rim's Grand Canyon Village and Desert View Watchtower. A short side route leads to **Point Imperial,** the highest overlook on the North Rim, with views of Mount Hayden and the Marble Platform.

Accommodations and Food

Built in 1928, the log-beam **◖ Grand Canyon Lodge** boasts two porches and an octagonal sunroom with huge windows to take advantage of the panorama. Cabins start at $120 per night, and it's a good idea to make reservations as far ahead of time as possible through Forever Resorts (888/386-4383, www.foreverlodging.com). The same goes for the **North**

© KATHLEEN BRYANT

The North Kaibab Trail leads into the depths of Grand Canyon.

Rim Campground (877/444-6777, www.recreation.gov) with sites for $18–25, showers, laundry facilities, a grocery, and a general store. The lodge restaurant (928/638-2611, ext. 760, $5–35) serves all meals, but reserve a table well in advance if you want to eat dinner while watching the sunset through the dining room's tall windows. Other options are the deli next to the lodge (all meals daily, $5–10) or the daily chuck-wagon cookout ($35 adults, $22 children).

Getting There
State Route 67, which originates at Jacob Lake, is the only paved route to the North Rim. U.S. 89A intersects SR 67 from the east (Marble Canyon area) and northwest (Fredonia/Kanab). Many North Rim visitors begin their trip to the North Rim from Las Vegas (275 miles), where it's easy to sign up for a tour or rent a car. You can also get there via the Trans Canyon Shuttle (928/638-2820, www.transcanyonshuttle.com, $150), which travels the

212 miles from the South Rim daily during summer months.

The nearest sizable city is St. George, Utah (156 miles). United and Delta fly into the St. George airport from Los Angeles and Salt Lake City. Flagstaff is 207 miles away, or about five hours.

The Kaibab Plateau
En route to the North Rim Entrance Station, U.S. 89A climbs into the cool evergreen forests of the Kaibab Plateau, and at almost 8,000 feet hits Jacob Lake, where it joins with SR 67. At the intersection, the **Jacob Lake Inn** (928/643-7232, www.jacoblake.com) has a year-round restaurant, rooms ($120–140), and cabins ($90–140). It's also where you'll find the **Kaibab Plateau Visitor Center** (928/643-7298, 8 A.M.–5 P.M. daily mid-May–mid-Oct., with shorter hours later in the season) run by the Forest Service.

Across the road, **Allen's Guided Tours** (Jacob Lake, 435/644-8150 or 435/689-1370, $15–75) organizes horseback trips into the Kaibab National Forest, and the Forest Service **Jacob Lake Campground** (928/643-7395, May 15–Nov. 1, depending on snowfall) has primitive sites for $17. A quarter mile south is the **Kaibab Camper Village** (928/643-7804 or 800/525-0924, May 15–Oct. 15, http://kaibabcampervillage.com) with full hookup sites ($35), tent sites ($17), and a cabin ($85). From there, SR 67 reaches almost 9,000 feet as it winds through the parklike meadows and pine-clad hills of the Kaibab National Forest, one of the prettiest in the lower 48. Buried by snow in winter, the road is open mid-May–mid-October, weather permitting.

Tuweep
For the adventurous, this "back door" to the North Rim of the Grand Canyon offers something that may seem unbelievable if you've ever been to the South Rim in tour-bus season: solitude. To get there you'll have to negotiate about 60 miles of dirt roads; don't try it with a low-slung car or when it's wet, and keep in mind that the Park Service recommends carrying not just one but two spare tires. From

Fredonia, drive seven miles west and turn off onto BLM Road 109 (the "Sunshine Route"), following the signs through BLM, wilderness, and ranch land to the Tuweep Ranger Station. It's another rough six miles to the campground. There aren't any tourist facilities (or water), but you can drive to the edge of the canyon and camp for free, often with only a handful of other people around. It's a whole other facet of the Grand Canyon, which looks more like a steep-walled gorge there, rather than a mountain range seen from above.

There are no barriers at this overlook and nothing between you and the 3,000-foot drop to the Colorado River. Far below is Lava Falls, the meanest rapid in the park: Sometimes you can hear it roar or see tiny rafts negotiating their way through the rocks. Eleven primitive campsites (first-come, first-served) are available near the rim, with picnic tables, fire grates, and composting toilets. Contact the park (928/638-7888, www.nps.gov/grca) for more information.

© KATHLEEN BRYANT

Tuweep is a remote area along Grand Canyon's northwest rim.

THE INNER CANYON

First, the warnings: Since it gets hotter as you descend into the gorge, and it typically takes twice as much time, energy, and water to climb back out, *and* it can hit over 100°F down there in summer, the inner canyon is as dangerous as it is beautiful. Don't go unprepared, gear- and fitness-wise. It's frighteningly easy to underestimate how challenging hiking in the Grand Canyon is. The combination of altitude, steep terrain, and lack of water claims victims every year.

The best times to venture into the canyon are in spring and fall; March, April, October, and November are ideal. From May to September, temperatures at the rim can be in the 90s and can climb to over 100°F in the canyon.

Permits are necessary for overnight camping in the backcountry ($10 plus $5 pp per night). These can be requested in person, by fax, or by mail, but be warned that the park receives about 20,000 requests every year and only grants 13,000. So apply early—up to four months ahead, on the first of the month. See the backcountry hiking portion of the park's website (www.nps.gov) for details and permit applications.

Hiking

From the South Rim, the **Bright Angel Trail** heads 9.3 miles downhill to **Phantom Ranch** at the river. A bunk in the men's or women's dorms is $42/night, and meals are also available. Reserve rooms through Xanterra Resorts (303/297-2757 or 888/297-2757, www.grand-canyonlodges.com). A wealth of other trails lead down into the gorge. One popular hike is the **Grandview Trail** from Grandview Point to Horseshoe Mesa, an old Indian route improved by miners more than a century ago (6 miles round-trip, strenuous).

From the North Rim, you can take the **North Kaibab Trail** (28 miles round-trip, strenuous) to Phantom Ranch. The steeper and more remote **Bill Hall Trail** also leads to the river (10 miles and 5,200 feet down). Near the bottom it passes **Thunder River,** which gushes out of a sheer limestone cliff before flowing right into the Colorado, making it by some estimates the shortest river in the world.

Rafting the Canyon

Riding the rapids of the Colorado River ranks high up on the list of Things You Should Do Before You Die. Follow in the footsteps of daring explorers as you hike up side canyons, float the placid stretches, and shrink in significance next to billions of years of geology. Unlike John Wesley Powell and other pioneer canyon adventurers, you'll enjoy gourmet meals and the (relative) luxury of sleeping bags on a sandy beach beneath the stars.

Commercial outfitters in Flagstaff and other regional cities offer many different options for guided river trips, and reservations are often available within months or even weeks. (In contrast, it can take years to win the lottery for a private trip permit.) Choose from motorized rafts, oar or paddle rafts, or classic hard-shell dories. The full 226 miles from Lees Ferry to Diamond Creek takes 11–19 days by oar or 6–8 days with a motor. Alternatively, you can join or leave a trip at Phantom Ranch, cutting your travel time considerably. The park's website (www.nps.gov/grca) includes a page on river trips, with links to outfitter/guides. Also helpful is the website of the **Grand Canyon River Outfitters Association** (www.gcroa.org).

Commercial outfitters include **Canyoneers** (928/526-0924 or 800/525-0924, www.canyoneers.com), which traces its origins to 1936, when Norman Nevills first guided a trip down the San Juan River. Their Grand Canyon offerings range from weeklong trips on motorized rafts ($1,959 pp) to 14-day excursions on oar boats ($3,250 pp). **Arizona Raft Adventures** (800/786-7238, www.azraft.com) offers motorized, paddle, oar, and hybrid Grand Canyon raft trips. If you need help sorting through the options, Tim and Pam Whitney have been running the Grand Canyon since 1973, and in 1986 they founded **Rivers and Oceans** (928/526-4575 or 800/473-4576, www.rivers-oceans.com). They provide a central reservation service for outfitted trips through the Grand Canyon, as well as trips on rivers in southern Utah and Idaho.

For those lucky souls who've landed a permit for a private river trip, planning and outfitting is easier with the services of a trip support company. **Canyon REO** (800/637-4604, www.canyonreo.com) has gear rentals, kayak instruction, meal planning, and shuttles.

Tours and Activities

Besides boot leather, another classic way to enter the canyon is on a **mule tour.** These sturdy animals have carried visitors up and down the canyon's trails for over a century. The Phantom Ranch mule tour (303/297-2757 or 888/297-2757, www.grandcanyonlodges.com, $482 one night, $674 two nights) departing from the South Rim is the only mule trip with an overnight in the canyon.

The **Grand Canyon Field Institute** (928/638-2485 or 866/471-4435, www.grandcanyon.org/fieldinstitute) organizes a wealth of guided educational overnight trips into the canyon March–November.

Helicopter tours over the canyon have been a contentious subject, with the machines' noise and intrusiveness jarring visitors who came to get away from it all. If you can't resist, **Maverick Helicopters** (928/638-2622 or 888/261-4414, www.maverickhelicopter.com) offers flights departing from the South Rim ($210–250 pp for 25–50 minutes).

Navajo Nation

At 27,000 square miles, the Big Rez (pop. 250,000) is larger than several U.S. states. Even so, the present-day reservation is smaller than Diné Bikeyah, the traditional Navajo homeland that stretched between the four sacred peaks: Sis Naajiní (Mount Blanco) in the east, Tsoodzil (Mount Taylor) to the south, Dook'o'oosliíd (the San Francisco Peaks) to the west, and Dibé Nitsaa (Mount Hesperus) in the north.

Four is an important number in Navajo cosmology. The Diné emerged from three previous worlds before entering this, the Fourth or Glittering World. The holy people—Spider Woman, Talking God, and others—arranged four sacred stones (black jet, white shell, turquoise, and abalone or coral) to mark tribal boundaries, and then placed the sun, moon, and stars and made clouds, trees, rain, and other necessities. The Navajo Nation flag and seal depict the four sacred mountains and their associated colors.

Though many Navajos work wage jobs today, tradition is strong in this land where landscape and culture are woven together as tightly as a Two Grey Hills rug. Ranching, herding, and farming are still central to the reservation economy. Artisans continue to produce silver and turquoise jewelry, though it's common now to see traditional craftsmanship applied to gold, sugalite, and other minerals. (By some estimates, 70 percent of the reservation's workers are associated with arts and crafts.) Hogans, traditional octagonal-shaped homes, still dot the landscape. Medicine men continue to conduct healing ceremonies, employing chant, sandpainting, and other techniques to restore *hozho,* or harmony.

A journey into Navajoland can encompass incredible scenery and fascinating history, from towering sandstone monuments and sculpted canyons to storied trading posts, where you can watch a rug weaver or listen to the Navajo language, famously used as a code by the U.S. military during World War II. A few of the reservation's scenic highlights—such as Monument Valley—are immediately recognizable across the world. Many other wonders are seldom seen by non-Navajos. Most are rich with cultural meaning or legend. Although Navajos graciously welcome visitors to the reservation, the tribe requires that non-Navajos obtain a pass ($5 pp per day) for camping, hiking, or backcountry explorations.

CAMERON AND VICINITY

The Navajo government is organized around 110 chapters, similar to counties or townships. The name for the Cameron chapter is Na ni' ah' hasani, which translates as "old structure across," in reference to the suspension bridge that crosses the Little Colorado River near the trading post. Cameron (pop. 1,200) is located on the reservation's western edge. There, the Painted Desert is a pastel landscape of rounded hills banded in lavender, rose, green, and gray. SR 64 meets U.S. 89 in Cameron, making this small community the gateway to the section of Grand Canyon's South Rim known as Desert View or the East Rim. The sprawling trading post complex north of the intersection is an interesting place to linger on the way to the Grand Canyon, Page, or Tuba City and the Hopi Mesas.

Sights

In 1911 a suspension bridge (named for Arizona Senator Ralph Cameron) was built over the Little Colorado River about 50 miles north of Flagstaff. Now closed, the **historic Cameron Suspension Bridge** is listed on the National Register. Five years later, Hubert and C. D. Richardson established a trading post where the Navajo and Hopi exchanged wool, blankets, and livestock for dry goods. Today the **Cameron Trading Post** (978/679-2231 or 800/338-7385, www.camerontradingpost. com) is employee-owned. The complex of stone buildings there—post, gallery, hotel, RV park—is a lovely enclave and a perfect home

THE LAUGHING PARTY

Part of Navajo tradition is the Chi Dlo Dil, or Laughing Party, held for newborns. At first, babies are considered to be of two worlds—the human world and the world of the holy people. The baby's laughter (at about six weeks) is a sign that the child is ready to be fully human and participate in the community. The first person to make the baby laugh, it is thought, will play an important role in the child's life. That person also is expected to host a feast, where friends and relatives gather to eat and play with the baby.

base for exploring the western reservation and the Grand Canyon.

Steep walls of Kaibab limestone and Coconino sandstone confine the Little Colorado River, dubbed the LCR or "Little C," to a narrow gorge on its final run to the Grand Canyon, where it joins the Colorado River. About 10 miles west of the Cameron junction, SR 64 edges the **Little Colorado River Gorge,** a Navajo Nation Tribal Park. The tribe charges a small entry fee to stop at the main overlook.

Shopping

The **Navajo Arts and Crafts Enterprise** (www.gonavajo.com) has represented regional artists since 1941, with five locations around the reservation. At the U.S. 89/SR 64 junction, NACE operates a store (928/679-2244) with jewelry, rugs, and other crafts.

The **Cameron Trading Post,** approximately a mile north of the U.S. 89/SR 64 junction, has a vast inventory of Native American art, from jewelry to rugs, but it also remains an active post where locals buy craft supplies and sundries and sell wool and piñon nuts. Make sure you don't miss the adjacent **gallery,** which has a museum-quality collection of antique and contemporary native art. Rugs, concho belts, pottery, kachina carvings, baskets, and Old West memorabilia fill the place from wooden floor

to wide-beamed ceiling. More pieces are on display upstairs, in a series of rooms restored to look like living quarters.

Roadside stands, like the ones at the Little Colorado River Gorge along SR 64, are places where you can purchase jewelry and other items directly from artists or their families.

Accommodations and Food

About a mile north of the intersection of U.S. 89 and SR 64, the **Cameron Trading Post** (reservations 800/338-7385) has an RV park ($25) and lodge with 66 rooms ($60–180) that feature hand-carved furniture and balcony views of the Little Colorado River. Many rooms are arranged around the hotel's lovely gardens, where Chinese elms, fruit trees, and rosebushes mingle with native plants. A large stone fireplace, pressed-tin ceiling, and gorgeously woven Navajo tapestries decorate the dining room, which serves all meals daily ($5–25).

Simpson's Market (928/679-2340), located at the junction of U.S. 89/SR 64, is a grocery with a deli serving sandwiches and other inexpensive bites.

Information and Services

Near the U.S. 89/SR 64 intersection, you'll find the **Cameron Visitor Center** (928/679-2303, www.navajonationparks.org), which provides information and issues permits for sites on the western Navajo Nation. Across the intersection is Simpson's convenience store and gas station. About a mile north at the Cameron Trading Post complex, you'll find gas pumps and a **post office.**

Grand Falls of the Little Colorado

In the spring (or after summer thunderstorms), chocolate-colored meltwater roars over the edge of this 185-foot cascade. The falls, which are higher than Niagara Falls, are about 50 miles northeast of Flagstaff at the edge of the San Francisco Volcanic Field. A tongue of lava from Merriam Crater created this pourover about 100,000 years ago. To get there, take exit 211 off I-40 east of Flagstaff and drive 2.3 miles north to Indian Route 15 (Leupp Road). Take IR 15 east 20 miles to the Grand Falls Bible

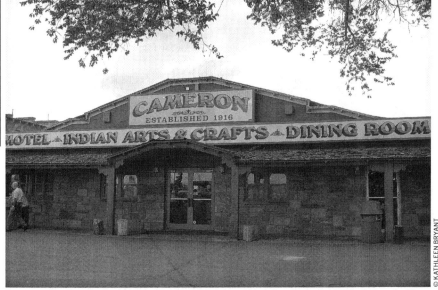

© KATHLEEN BRYANT

Cameron Trading Post combines shopping, dining, and lodging along the Little Colorado River.

Church sign, between mileposts 5 and 6. Turn left onto a dirt road that ends at the falls overlook, about 9.5 miles. A high-clearance vehicle is recommended. In the spring or after a storm, when the falls are running, the dirt road can be muddy and impassable. For those planning to do any hiking in the area, the Cameron Visitor Center (928/679-2303, 8 A.M.–5 P.M. Mon.–Fri., hours vary seasonally), at the junction of U.S. 89/SR 64, is the nearest parks office issuing permits.

TUBA CITY AND VICINITY

One of the Navajo Reservation's most diverse communities, Tuba City (pop. 8,500) sits off U.S. 89 between Flagstaff and Page, about 45 miles northwest of the Hopi Mesas. The Navajo name for Tuba City is To'Nanees'Dizi (Water Scattered). Mormon settlers called it Tuba City after a Hopi chief called Tuuvi, who established the nearby village of Moenkopi as a summer farming community in the 1870s.

Tuuvi was the first Hopi to meet Brigham Young, and after converting to the Mormon faith, Tuuvi donated a plot of land to the church on the condition that Mormon settlers would protect the Hopi from Navajo and Paiute raiders. Moenave was a small spring-fed oasis west of Tuba City along the Honeymoon Trail. Trailblazer Jacob Hamblin established a settlement there, and it became a popular stop for Mormon couples traveling between their Little Colorado River farms and St. George, Utah, the nearest temple where wedding vows could be solemnized. The last Latter-Day Saint left Moenave near the turn of the 20th century, when the area was added to the Navajo Reservation.

The Hopi village of Moenkopi, "the place of running water," sits across SR 264 from Tuba City. From there, Moenkopi Wash cuts across the desert to the Hopi Mesas. Hopis who farmed at Moenkopi would run between their fields and their home village of Oraibi—a distance of over 30 miles—several times a week.

The Navajo Reservation, like much of the United States, observes daylight saving time. The Hopi Reservation, like the rest of Arizona,

NAVAJO CRAFTS

The Diné tell how Spider Woman taught their ancestors to weave on looms built by her husband. The introduction of curly-horned Churro sheep by the Spanish in the 17th century, along with the adoption of pueblo-style looms as well as a more sedentary lifestyle, allowed the tribe to become expert weavers. Today their **rugs** can hold their own among the world's finest handmade textiles. Women traditionally own the sheep and weave the rugs, which can take months to make. (The Churro sheep had almost become extinct by the 1970s but is being pulled back from the brink through a process of careful breeding.)

Navajo rugs combine Mexican and Spanish stylistic influences with geometric designs and representations of natural phenomena. At the advice of early Anglo traders, the weavers expanded their repertoire to include more intricate patterns. True Navajo rugs are woven from sheep wool, and a quick sniff will reveal an earthy aroma. Other things to look for in a quality rug include symmetry, straight edges, coloration, and a tight, flat weave. You'll often find a "spirit line" running to the border, included to keep the weaver's spirit from being trapped inside the pattern.

Styles include the geometric Two Grey Hills, made of natural white, gray, and brown wool; the pastel vegetals (plant-based dyes) of the Burnt Water style; the elaborately banded Wide Ruins; and the self-explanatory Eye Dazzlers and Pictorials. Some rug patterns are identified by their colors, such as Ganado (deep red) and Klagetoh (gray). Yei rugs depict the Holy People, and Yeibichai illustrate ceremonies in which the Holy People are impersonated by human dancers. Prices range anywhere from the low hundreds to well into the thousands, with a quality 3-by-5-foot rug generally going for about $500-750. This is an exacting art and, sadly, a dying one, since fewer young weavers are learning the old techniques. For this reason, a quality rug will hold its price well and probably even climb in value. Good rugs will also last for years—some old ones have endured over a century of boot traffic.

The Navajos originally learned the technique of **silversmithing** from Mexican smiths, and by the 1860s the craft was spreading throughout the region. Early Navajo silver was made from silver coins, but traders began stocking materials and tools, and smiths expanded their repertoire. By the early 1900s Navajo silver encompassed chunky bracelets, elaborately detailed concha belts, rings inlaid with turquoise and coral, and gorgeous "squash blossom" necklaces. Traditional Navajo silver jewelry is often sand- or tufa-cast, polished to a bright luster, and die-stamped with decorative details. Navajo matriarchs still go out in their best necklaces and bracelets, with enough turquoise to ransom a princess. Men wear the *ketoh* (bow guard), a wide forearm band that is now purely decorative. Turquoise remains the most common stone, but new techniques have seen the addition of gold and a veritable rainbow of precious and semiprecious stones.

Navajo **sandpaintings** re-create the ceremonial designs drawn on hogan floors by medicine men, which are gathered and scattered to the winds when the ritual is finished. Sandpaintings are drawn with glue on plywood or particleboard and then sprinkled with minerals collected on the reservation. Look for precise workmanship, and know that you're not getting a true religious artifact—small details are changed in the paintings to avoid offending the Holy People.

One of the most widely recognized types of baskets made in the Southwest is the Navajo **ceremonial basket,** a wide, shallow dish woven of sumac and mahogany fibers. These baskets are made using a concentric coil technique and have geometric designs in muted colors. They are most commonly used in traditional weddings.

Tribe members produce many other types of crafts and fine arts. These include pottery, leatherwork, wood carvings, ceramic and alabaster sculpture, **"folk art"** (figurines carved from wood or fashioned from clay), oil or acrylic paintings, drums, cedar flutes, stained glass, and furniture.

does not. Thus, when you cross the highway between Tuba City and Moenkopi during summer months, you change time zones. Keep this in mind when you are traveling from one area to the next.

Although predominantly Navajo, Tuba City has many residents who belong to the Hopi and other tribes, as well as Anglos. The Bashas' grocery store (928/283-5250), at the junction of SR 160/SR 264, serves as the unofficial community gathering place. Though many travelers zip past without a second glance on their way to Page or the North Rim, the oasis of Tuba City makes an interesting and pleasant stop en route to the Hopi Mesas.

Sights

Next to the Tuba City Trading Post, the **Explore Navajo Interactive Museum** (Main St. and Moenave Rd., 928/283-5441, 8 A.M.–6 P.M. Mon.–Sat., noon–6 P.M. Sun., $9 adults, $6 children) holds exhibits on the tribe's history and culture, including crafts and the Navajo Code Talkers of WWII.

Tuba City sits on a mesa north of U.S. 160 in one of the most striking expanses of the **Painted Desert.** About two miles east on U.S. 160 from U.S. 89, a dirt turnoff leads to the top of a small hill, a great place to take photos and enjoy the view.

Three more miles brings you to another turnoff marked by a hand-lettered sign for **Moenave,** the site of the original Mormon settlement. Near the turnoff are a set of **dinosaur tracks** laid down by the nine-foot Dilophosaurus in the late Triassic mud. Navajo children are usually on hand to give you a short tour (a small tip is expected) and will point out the three-toed footprints, petrified eggs, and even an embedded claw. The settlement of Moenave itself, at the base of Hamblin Ridge, is a green oasis fed by springs. John D. Lee, of Lees Ferry, hid out there for a while before being tracked down and executed for his role in the Mountain Meadows Massacre.

Fifteen miles southeast of Tuba City along SR 264, beautiful **Coal Mine Canyon** secrets a collection of colorful hoodoos and cliffs.

This treasure is easy to miss: The canyon is less than a mile long, and there are no signs to indicate its presence on the barren landscape. Look for a dirt road leading to a windmill between mile markers 336 and 337. The Navajo call this serrated landscape *hááhonoojí* (jagged), and the Hopi tell of Quayowuuti, the Eagle Woman from Old Oraibi who stepped from the edge of the canyon to her death. Her ghost is said to appear under the full moon. Permits for visiting and hiking the canyon are available at the Cameron Visitor Center (928/679-2303, 8 A.M.–5 P.M. Mon.–Fri., hours vary seasonally), at the junction of U.S. 89/SR 64 in Cameron.

Red Lake Trading Post (928/283-5194) also known as Tonalea Trading Post, is 20 miles northwest of Tuba City along U.S. 160. The building dates to 1891, when the Babbitt Brothers Trading Company built it using Arbuckle coffee boxes for some of the walls. The post has a rich and storied history, including being the scene of a tragic love triangle and appearing in Zane Grey's novel *Rainbow Trail.* It was used as a location for *The Dark Wind* (1991), based on the Tony Hillerman novel and produced by Robert Redford. Today it's a convenience market where you can stop and get a cool drink before continuing your drive. A mile north, you'll see the **Elephant Feet,** a pair of stocky sandstone pillars on the west side of the highway.

Shopping and Events

The **Tuba City Trading Post** (10 N. Main, 928/283-5441), established in 1870, was operated for a time by the Babbitt family. Teddy Roosevelt stayed there in 1913 on his way back from hunting mountain lions on the North Rim of the Grand Canyon, and Zane Grey also visited. The present octagonal-shaped building was constructed in the 1930s out of local blue limestone with logs from the San Francisco Peaks. Today the trading post displays a wealth of quality crafts, including Navajo rugs woven in the bold geometric storm pattern developed in the Tuba City area.

Every Friday the **Tuba City Flea Market**

coalesces behind the chapter house. A little bit of everything is for sale—car parts, used clothing, medicinal herbs, turquoise jewelry—and when you need a break from browsing, you can listen to the lilting sounds of the Navajo language over a bowl of mutton stew and fry bread.

The **Western Navajo Fair** is held every October on the first weekend after Columbus Day. Make hotel reservations early if you plan to attend this popular event, which includes a rodeo, beauty pageant, dances, and a Yeibichei ceremony.

Accommodations and Food

At the intersection of U.S. 160 and SR 264, the recently completed **Moenkopi Legacy Inn & Suites** (928/283-4500, http://experiencehopi. com, $100–220) has 100 rooms and suites with amenities that include a pool and fitness center. It's one of only two hotels on Hopi tribal land, and the lobby, anchored by a three-story fireplace designed by Eddie Calnimptewa, showcases their art and culture. Next to the Tuba City Trading Post, the **Quality Inn** (928/283-4545, 10 N. Main, $120–165) has a restaurant and an RV park with six tent sites. Students at the Greyhills Academy High School run the 32-room **Greyhills Inn** (U.S. 160 and Warrior Dr., 928/283-6271, ext. 142, $62) as part of a training program in hotel management.

Dining options are limited in Tuba City. At the U.S. 160/SR 264 intersection, the **Tuuvi Café** (928/283-4374, all meals daily, $5–10) serves American food and a few Hopi dishes like hominy stew. Drive north along SR 264 and you'll spot a handful of chains, as well as the **Hogan Restaurant** (928/283-5260, all meals daily, $5–15) at the Quality Inn, serving American and Mexican dishes with a few local specialties and a salad bar.

KAYENTA AND VICINITY

The largest city (pop. 5,000) in the northern part of the Navajo Reservation takes its name, loosely, from the Navajo *teehindeeh*, meaning "bog hole" or "natural game pit," after the glue-like soil around a nearby spring that mired livestock. The Navajo also call it Tódíneeshzheé, meaning "water spreading out like fingers."

Once the center of the Ancestral Puebloan world, Kayenta is now a dusty town of pickup trucks and cowboy hats, home to miners and farmers. Kayenta's chief attraction is its access to nearby Navajo National Monument and Monument Valley Tribal Park, and it makes a convenient stop en route to Four Corners National Monument. You'll find a few motels, inexpensive restaurants, and a shopping center at the intersection of U.S. 160 and 163.

There, as elsewhere in Navajo country, landscape and story are inseparable. As you drive U.S. 160 northeast, you'll parallel **Comb Ridge,** a 100-mile-long sandstone monocline that Navajos say represents the earth's backbone. Across the highway north of town is a cluster of hoodoos known as **Baby Rocks Mesa.** One of the reddish spires is said to be a girl who refused to share bread with a baby sister. The Holy People turned her into stone, and she stands today as a warning against selfishness.

Views encompass diatremes, or volcanic necks, thrusting up from the high desert floor. One of these, **Aglatha Peak,** is located along U.S. 163, marking the gateway to Monument Valley. Among the many stories associated with this peak is one identifying it as the center of the world, where the Holy People propped up the sky. Kit Carson renamed it El Capitan when he rode through there in his 1863–64 campaign against the Navajos.

Sights

The Navajos have a long, proud warrior tradition, and many young men volunteered for military service during World War II. Some 400 were trained as Code Talkers and sworn to secrecy about their roles in order to preserve the code. It wasn't until 1968, when the U.S. government declassified their story, that their unique contributions to the war were acknowledged. Another 30-odd years passed before the Code Talkers were officially honored with Congressional Medals of Honor, awarded at a ceremony in 2001. Inside the Burger King restaurant, located just west of the U.S. 160/U.S. 163 intersection, one wall is dedicated to an exhibit of letters, uniform parts, and other artifacts relating to the **Navajo Code Talkers.**

Next door to the restaurant, the **Navajo Cultural Center** (928/697-3170) has examples of male and female hogans and the Shadehouse Museum, which displays additional Code Talker memorabilia. The shadehouse was built by Richard Mike, whose father was a Code Talker.

Shopping and Events

Crafts, Western wear, and craft supplies are sold at the **Navajo Arts and Crafts Enterprises** (928/697-8611, 9 A.M.–6 P.M. Mon.–Fri. spring–fall, with limited weekend hours in winter) near the U.S. 160/U.S. 163 intersection. The **Kayenta Fourth of July Rodeo** is a hugely popular multi-day event with live Western music and fireworks.

Accommodations and Food

Kayenta has only a few chain hotels, all near the intersection of U.S. 160 and 163, including the **Best Western Wetherill Inn** (928/697-3231, $80–140) and the **Holiday Inn** (928/697-3221, $90–170).

At the main intersection, the **Blue Coffee Pot** (928/697-3396, 6 A.M.–9 P.M. Mon.–Fri.) is a local favorite, serving good steaks, Mexican, and Navajo dishes for $5–9. About 10 miles west on U.S. 160, the Hampton Inn's **Reuben Heflin Restaurant** (928/697-3170, dinner daily) serves seafood, steak, and Southwestern cuisine.

NAVAJO NATIONAL MONUMENT

Twenty miles southwest of Kayenta, this small national monument protects two of the most impressive and intact prehistoric pueblos in the Four Corners. The monument lies within the Navajo Reservation on the Shonto Plateau, nine miles off U.S. 160 at the end of SR 564. The ruins, both cliff dwellings, are open for visitation. Start at the **visitors center** (928/672-2700, www.nps.gov/nava, 8 A.M.–6 P.M. Memorial Day–Labor Day, otherwise 9 A.M.–5 P.M., free), which has a museum and bookstore. Local Navajo artists demonstrate their crafts there on occasion. The monument observes daylight saving time.

Sights and Hikes

Two short, easy trails lead along the canyon rim

to overlooks of **Betatakin** (Navajo for "ledge house"), a 125-room pueblo tucked into a dramatically arched stone alcove. The only way to experience this cliff dwelling up close is to take a ranger-led tour, offered from spring through fall. The five-mile round-trip tour requires some effort—the trail is sandy and steep, like walking up the stairs of a 70-story building at 7,300-foot elevation—but it's worth every sweaty step.

The Betatakin tour departs twice daily on summer mornings. Allow three–five hours for the strenuous hike, which can be particularly trying in summer heat. (Tours are available on some winter weekends, depending on staffing.)

Keet Seel (Navajo for "broken pottery") is more than eight miles from the visitors center, meaning you can spend a night at the small, primitive campground near the ruin or do the whole 17-mile round trip in an epic one-day push. Either way, you'll be able to follow a ranger through this 100-room settlement tucked under a cliff overhang. Only a handful of visitors are allowed on each tour, and the experience is haunting: Decorated potsherds and corncobs lie scattered around the silent village, and wood ladders and beams poke out of masonry rooms, as though the inhabitants simply walked away and never returned. Many archaeologists consider it among the best-preserved Southwestern ruins.

Accommodations and Food

The monument has two free **campgrounds,** one with 31 sites and another with 11 sites. The closest lodgings are in Tsegi Canyon, about 14 miles southeast on U.S. 160. The **Anasazi Inn** (928/697-3793) has 57 rooms ($95–120) and a small café serving all meals daily. The rooms and menu are simple, but you can't beat the setting in the pink sandstone gorge.

◖ MONUMENT VALLEY TRIBAL PARK

Drive north of Kayenta on U.S. 163 toward the Utah border, and you may feel like you've entered a Western movie sunset just as the credits started to roll. Rising from the flat plain like

© KATHLEEN BRYANT

Betatakin is one of the cliff dwellings preserved at Navajo National Monument.

the gods' own rock garden, the stone monoliths of Monument Valley are the unmistakable icon of the American West, recognizable worldwide, thanks to countless movies, television commercials, and photographs. Director John Ford, the first to put Monument Valley on the big screen, called it the "most complete, beautiful, and peaceful place on earth."

The Navajo consider all of Tsébii'nidzisgai (the "valley within the rocks") to be one huge hogan, with the traditional east-facing door situated near the visitors center. Chief Hoskininni led many Navajos to the valley for refuge there during Kit Carson's scorched earth campaign of 1863–64, and about 100 people still live and farm there. The valley became the Navajos' first tribal park in 1958. Visitation is limited to a single loop road and permitted tours. (Rock climbing there—or elsewhere on the reservation—is forbidden, regardless of what you saw in *The Eiger Sanction* or *Vertical Limit*.)

The floor of Monument Valley is a weathered, river-deposited siltstone laid down more than 200 million years ago. Iron oxide within the siltstone gives it a reddish color. Over the millennia, the softer siltstone has eroded, revealing vertically jointed slabs of sandstone in the form of massive buttes and spires with names like Totem Pole, the Yei Bi Chei, the Three Sisters, and the Mittens. Many Monument Valley formations are capped by harder Moenkopi shale and Shinarump. Dark, jagged peaks on the valley's southern edge are volcanic remnants.

Visiting Monument Valley

At an intersection on the state line, a short road leads east to the **Monument Valley Navajo Tribal Park** (435/727-5870, www. navajonationparks.org, 6 A.M.–8 P.M. daily, 8 A.M.–5 P.M. Oct.–Apr., $5 pp). The recently constructed hotel and visitors center complex is at the edge of the valley, situated to take in the glorious view from large windows and a multilevel terrace. The visitors center has exhibits on Navajo culture and a gift shop with native crafts, books, and souvenirs.

From there, the 17-mile, self-guided **loop**

road descends into the valley, past many Navajo homes and a viewing point named for director John Ford. Allow at least two hours for the dirt road, which is suitable for most two-wheel-drive vehicles and closes shortly before sundown. It's also a great mountain bike ride.

If you'd prefer to sit back and enjoy while someone else does the driving, or if you'd like to get off the main road, dozens of local operators offer guided trail rides, hikes, and vehicle tours. One of them, **Sacred Monument Tours** (435/727-3218, www.monumentvalley.net), has hiking, jeep, and horseback riding tours starting at $70, with an all-day horseback-riding tour for $300 per person. Longer tours leave the loop road for backcountry petroglyphs and ruins. **Roland's Navajoland Tours** (928/697-3524) leads Monument Valley tours out of Kayenta.

For the classic road-trip shot of Monument Valley—the place where Forrest Gump finally stopped running—approach from the north on U.S. 163, the **Monument Valley-Bluff Scenic Byway.** A little more than 13 miles north of the Utah-Arizona border there's a small hill, with the highway heading straight as an arrow toward the valley below: You'll recognize the view.

Adjacent to the visitors center, the recently opened **View Hotel** (435/727-5555, www.monumentvalleyview.com, $150–300) has rooms with balconies overlooking the valley's formations, a deli counter, and a restaurant serving all meals daily. The aptly named hotel is often fully booked months in advance by tour companies during peak season, but cancellations are possible. Nearby is access to the **Wildcat Trail** (four miles round-trip), which circumnavigates one of the Mittens and is the only park trail where non-Navajos can hike without an authorized guide.

Mitten View Campground sits at the edge of the valley near the visitors center. Of its 100 campsites, sites 24 and 25 have the best views, making it well worth getting up for sunrise. Group, tent, and RV sites are available ($10, no hookups) year-round, with restrooms and coin-operated showers open in high season.

The View Hotel sits on the edge of Monument Valley.

Goulding's Lodge and Trading Post

At the north end of the valley at the Arizona-Utah state line is a trading post established in a 10-person tent by Harry Goulding and his wife, Mike, in the 1920s. Harry, called **Dibé Nééz** ("Tall Sheep") by the Navajo, purchased 640 acres at the base of Black Door Mesa in 1937 for $320. Goulding bought local crafts, settled disputes, and acted as a liaison between the Navajo and the government. Hoping to bring jobs to the area during the Great Depression, he traveled to Hollywood to persuade director John Ford that the local scenery would make an ideal movie location. The rest is celluloid history. Monument Valley has been the backdrop for countless movies, including the classic Westerns *Stagecoach* (1939), *My Darling Clementine* (1946), and *Fort Apache* (1948). As Hollywood started to arrive, the Gouldings opened a lodge that became a second home to stars like John Wayne. Movie memorabilia and trading-post artifacts fill the original trading post, which has been turned into a museum (open daily year-round). A suggested donation of $2 is put toward scholarships for local children.

The modern **lodge** (435/727-3231, www.gouldings.com) has 62 rooms ($80–200) and the Stagecoach Dining Room, built for the filming of *She Wore a Yellow Ribbon* (1949). You can rent a Western movie to watch in your room . . . or just gaze from your balcony at the real thing. A year-round **campground** has views of the valley as well, with cabins ($80–100) or sites for tents ($25) and RVs ($44). Amenities include a coin laundry, hot showers, and shuttles to the lodge's heated indoor pool, grocery store, and dining room. Sign up at the lodge for Navajo-guided **tours** to nearby ruins, petroglyphs, crafts demonstrations, and movie locations.

Oljato

Eight miles past Goulding's, the **Oljato Trading Post** was opened in 1905 by cowboy archaeologist John Wetherill. The present building was constructed in 1921 and served the local population for decades before closing its doors. Once, more than 150 posts dotted the Navajo reservation. Locals depended on trading posts until highways improved, automobiles replaced horse travel, and distant regional shopping centers offered a greater variety of goods at lower prices. Of the handful of posts remaining in business today, most have modernized by adding gas pumps and tourist conveniences. Oljato is a fine example of a traditional post—simply built and remotely located. Though you can no longer see the interior of the low-roofed stone building, the drive there is well worth it for the scenery and ambiance.

◀ CANYON DE CHELLY NATIONAL MONUMENT

Joseph Campbell, international guru of mythology, once called this canyon system in northeast Arizona "the most sacred place on earth." The four canyons there—del Muerto, Black Rock, de Chelly, and Monument canyons—sheltered Ancestral Puebloan farmers, and later, acted as a Navajo stronghold. Navajos consider this to be the spiritual heart of Diné Bikeyah, the traditional homeland bounded by the four sacred mountains.

Covering 130 square miles of precipitous gorges and fertile canyon bottoms, Canyon de Chelly (de-SHAY) has the ageless quality of a place inhabited for thousands of years, and Navajo families continue to farm and tend orchards and herds of animals beneath its soaring sandstone cliffs. Navajo families still own the land that comprises the monument, which is administered by the National Park Service. Roads run along the north and south rims, with sweeping overlooks that take in rock spires, ancient ruins, and farmland. Aside from a single trail to the bottom, the only way to visit the canyon depths is to join a Navajo-led tour.

The canyon rims range 5,000–7,000 feet in elevation. Down the center runs the Rio de Chelly, from its beginnings in the Chuska Mountains in the east to the mouth of Canyon de Chelly near the town of Chinle, meaning "the place where the water flows out." The glowing red sandstone walls are over 1,000 feet high in places and as sheer as the side of a skyscraper. Temperatures range from well below 0°F in winter to over 100°F in summer, but the river-deposited sediments and reliable water supply make the canyon bottom excellent for farming. Side streams dry up in summer and rage with flash floods during the summer rainy seasons and spring snowmelt. Quicksand is often a concern in wet, sandy spots.

History

The earliest people to shelter in this canyon system were nomadic bands, who camped seasonally in alcoves while hunting game and foraging plants. Beginning about 2,500 years ago, during what is known as the Basketmaker Phase, people began experimenting with agriculture. They pecked hand-and-foot trails in cliff faces and progressed from dispersed jacal shelters and pit houses to impressive multiroom cliff dwellings cultivating canyon bottoms. Around A.D. 1300, Ancestral Puebloan villagers migrated from the canyon, joining other clans to establish pueblos near the Little Colorado River.

Their descendants, the Hopis, farmed Canyon de Chelly sporadically thereafter, and members of other tribes fled there after the Pueblo Revolt of 1680, but by 1700 Navajos were using the canyons and upland plateaus. The Navajo families who settled there brought livestock and peach trees introduced by the Spanish, having learned farming techniques and weaving from the pueblo tribes. They called the canyons Tséyi', meaning "within the rocks," but it is the Spanish mispronunciation of the word that has stuck.

For more than a century, the canyons' cornfields and peach orchards were a refuge from repeated raiding between various tribes and Spanish colonists. The Navajos fortified the canyons with stone walls, hidden trails, and food caches. Even so, Spanish, Ute, and later U.S. military parties occasionally managed to get past the defenses. Some of these attacks are memorialized by pictographs painted or drawn on the canyon walls.

Beginning in 1863 Kit Carson's merciless campaign drove hundreds of Navajos from their homes. Soldiers entered this canyon stronghold in the winter of 1864, killing or capturing those sheltered there, later destroying orchards and hogans and slaughtering livestock so that any survivors could not return. Those who survived the assault were forced on the Long Walk to eastern New Mexico, where they were incarcerated for four years before being allowed to return to a reservation established by treaty in 1868.

The canyons were declared a national monument in 1931, under a rare arrangement in which management is shared by the tribe and the National Park Service. The Navajo still grow melons, corn, beans, and squash on the fertile canyon bottom, where sheep and goats wander among cottonwoods and peach orchards.

Visiting Canyon de Chelly

Just east of the town of Chinle, the sandstone cliffs lower to about 30 feet, forming a natural gateway to the canyon system. You can take the rough road leading into the canyons only if you're on a guided tour or if you're a resident. Three miles east of Chinle, the **visitors center** (928/674-5500, www.nps.gov/cach, 8 A.M.–5 P.M. daily) has exhibits on the area's history and geology, as well as restrooms and drinking water. Entrance to the monument is free. Navajo Parks and Recreation charges a small fee for **Cottonwood Campground** (928/674-2106), open year-round. (The campground doesn't have hookups and can't accommodate RVs longer than 40 feet.) Nearby is the beautiful **Thunderbird Lodge** (just inside the park entrance on South Rim Drive, 928/674-5841 or 800/679-2473, www.tbirdlodge.com), which began as a trading post built by Sam Day in 1902. The original post building is now the cafeteria, decorated with Navajo rugs and open for all meals daily, featuring fry bread, chili, and other inexpensive Navajo and American dishes. The lodge is open year-round, with 73 rooms ($115–171). Rates drop by almost half in winter months. The lodge has a fine gift shop and offers half- and full-day canyon excursions ($52–83) in Unimogs, dubbed "shake-and-bake" tours by locals.

Canyon de Chelly's four main gorges and numerous side canyons slice generally eastward into the Defiance Plateau. Narrow paved roads parallel the northern and southern edges of the canyon system, where overlooks offer fantastic views of rock formations and ruins tucked into shadowy alcoves. Short trails lead to the cliff edges. Be careful at the overlooks: There are sharp drop-offs and the occasional car theft; don't leave anything of value in plain view.

North Rim Drive

This 17-mile section of Indian Route (IR) 64, which connects Chinle to Diné College and Tsaile, runs along Canyon del Muerto, Spanish for "Canyon of the Dead" (also referred to as North Canyon by locals). Archaeology buffs will find this drive especially interesting for its combination of tribal history, rock art, and well-preserved ruins. At the first of four overlooks, you can see 900-year-old Ledge Ruin and—if your eyes are sharp—a line of toeholds leading to a separate room.

At seven miles is **Antelope House Overlook,** above a ruin named for pictographs of running antelopes painted by a Navajo artist around 1830. The ruins and pictographs left by Ancestral Puebloans are at least 1,000 years older. Directly across the canyon, above the junction of Canyon del Muerto and Black Rock Canyon to the south, is the **Navajo Fortress,** an aerie where Navajo warriors hid from attackers, sneaking down at night for water and food.

Drive another nine miles, turn right, and take the right-hand fork for **Mummy Cave Overlook,** named by archaeologist Earl Morris for two mummified corpses found below. The ruins, thought to have been occupied between A.D. 300 and 1300, are situated in two cliff alcoves with a three-story Mesa Verde–style tower in between. The left-hand fork leads to **Massacre Cave Overlook.** When Lieutenant Antonio de Narbona led a punitive expedition into the canyon in 1805 to quell Navajo raids, the Spaniards found a group hiding in this cave. Over the course of two days, Spanish riflemen killed 115 people in the cave by bouncing bullets off its ceiling from the rim above. The bones of the victims remain in the cave untouched, per Navajo custom. It's a short walk to **Yucca Cave Overlook,** where you can see a small cliff dwelling and granary, connected by a series of toeholds.

South Rim Drive

This road parallels Canyon de Chelly (also called South Canyon), with views of the Chuska Mountains as well as the canyon system. You can stop at the **Tunnel Overlook** and **Tsegi Overlook** for views of the lower canyon and farms en route to **Junction Overlook,** about four miles from the visitors center. There, Canyon del Muerto joins Canyon de Chelly, and the rim is less than 500 feet above the creek. **First Ruin** and **Junction Ruin** are both visible.

It's another two miles to **White House Overlook,** which offers not only a great view but also the only way to reach the canyon bottom without a guide. The steep, rocky trail down to **White House Ruin** (2.5 miles round-trip, easy) descends 600 feet, passing through short tunnels and near a farm and orchard before crossing the wash on a footbridge. The trail ends in front of the well-preserved upper and lower ruins, named for the white-painted plaster finish on one of the rooms. Long streaks of desert varnish (manganese oxide) extend from the rim to the alcove, making this site a favorite of photographers. Nearby, you'll find restrooms and Navajo vendors selling jewelry and other items. Bring plenty of water, as the trail is sun-exposed. Respect the privacy of the families living in the canyon; don't wander off the trail without a guide.

Drive six more miles for the turnoff to **Sliding House Overlook.** The ruins there are named for the sloping alcove floor. A couple of miles farther along South Rim Drive is the **Spider Rock Campground** (928/674-8261, www.spiderrockcampground.com). Owned by local resident Howard Smith, this year-round campground has tent sites for $10 and RV sites for $15, as well as solar-heated showers and two hogans starting at $30. At **Face Rock Overlook,** twenty miles east of the visitors center, the canyon rims are now 1,000 feet above the wash. The ruins there are named for the stone spire nearby.

Follow the paved road northeast another mile, where it ends at **Spider Rock Overlook,** the park's most outstanding viewing point. An 800-foot rock tower thrusts from the canyon bottom where three canyons come together, one of the most breathtaking sights in the Southwest. Navajos call this monolith Tse' Na' ashjé'ii and tell of the supernatural being who lives on top. Spider Woman teaches weaving on a loom whose warp is the rays of the sun. Navajo mothers once warned their children to behave or else Spider Woman would carry them to her perch, said to be white with bones.

Tours

Canyon de Chelly Unimog Tours (928/674-5433, www.canyondechellytours.com) offers tours of the canyon bottom in jeeps, the military-looking, natural-gas powered Unimog, or your own vehicle. Tours start at $66 adults ($44 children) for a half day. They can also organize an overnight campout in the canyon.

Authorized Navajo guides offer driving tours (your vehicle—high-clearance, 4WD recommended) for $15 per hour. They lead hiking tours (15 people maximum) for the same price—an absolute bargain granting access to some of the canyon's most amazing historical and scenic treasures. Ask at the visitors center for details and trail suggestions. Some local residents, including James Yazzie, Jr. (928/674-5647), can arrange for overnight treks or horseback tours.

Chinle

The town of Chinle (pop. 5,300), situated at the mouth of Canyon de Chelly, is surrounded by farms and ranches, making it a busy shopping hub for rural residents. At Bashas' grocery store, look for labels in Navajo. For jewelry and other crafts, try the **Navajo Arts & Crafts Enterprises** at the main intersection. The Chinle area is known for cross-banded rugs woven with wool in vegetal dyes, though other styles are also woven there. The Chinle Comprehensive Health Care Facility (928/674-7001) combines traditional Navajo healing practices with modern medicine; it

even includes a hogan for ceremonies. Food and accommodation can be found at **Best Western** (100 Main St., 928/674-5874), with 100 rooms for $110, and a **Holiday Inn** (928/674-5000, from $115), close to the canyon on IR 7 at the site of the Garcia trading post. Both have heated pools and restaurants open daily for all meals, and both offer bargain winter rates.

HUBBELL TRADING POST NATIONAL HISTORIC SITE

The oldest continuously operating trading post on the Navajo Reservation was built on the banks of Pueblo Colorado Wash in 1871. Clerk and interpreter John Lorenzo Hubbell bought the post seven years later, and it stayed in his family until the National Park Service purchased it in 1965. Over the decades, Hubbell built one of the most successful trading empires in the Southwest, buying out and opening other posts throughout the Four Corners and earning the nickname Don Lorenzo, a Spanish term of respect, for his fair dealing and hospitality.

Hubbell learned the Navajos' culture and language, counseling them and treating their sick during an 1886 smallpox epidemic. He advised weavers on which designs would fetch the best prices. (The handsome Ganado pattern, with its deep red wool and cross motif, is still woven.) He brought a silversmith from Mexico to teach the art to locals. The Hubbells—Lorenzo, his wife, Lina, Rubi, and their four children—amassed one of the largest art collections in the Southwest in their home next to the post.

Today the original 160-acre homestead, one mile west of Ganado on SR 264, is administered by the National Park Service (928/755-3475, www.nps.gov/hutr, 8 A.M.–6 P.M. May–early Sept., until 5 P.M. in winter, free). The old trading post is operated by the Western National Parks Association (928/755-3254, www.wnpa.org). The post still buys and sells crafts, food, and supplies, though most sales now are to tourists. The rug room in back boasts a king's ransom in Navajo textiles.

© KATHLEEN BRYANT

Hubbell Trading Post is the oldest continuously operated post on the Navajo Reservation.

Demonstrations and auctions of Native American crafts are held throughout the year, and daily tours take visitors into the Hubbell home ($2 pp), which has retained all its original furnishings, excluding rugs. The ceiling in the main hallway is covered with dozens of woven baskets, and works by artists who visited the family adorn the walls, including portraits by Maynard Dixon and E. A. Burbank done with red Conté crayon.

WINDOW ROCK

The administrative center of the Navajo Nation straddles the New Mexico–Arizona border 24 miles northwest of Gallup on Highway 264/3. Window Rock (pop. 3,000) owes its importance to John Collier, commissioner of Indian Affairs in the 1930s, who brought the reservation's various offices together there as the Navajo Central Agency. He is remembered for his sympathetic ear in matters such as the tribe's education and health care, including the replacing of boarding schools with day schools for children.

Sights

The **Navajo Nation Museum** (928/871-7941, 8 A.M.–5 P.M. Mon.–Fri., until 8 P.M. Wed., 9 A.M.–5 P.M. Sat., free) is near the intersection of SR 264 and IR 12. The museum has well-done displays on tribal history, geology, and archaeology. Sharing the same parking lot are the **Navajo Parks & Recreation Department** (928/871-6647, www.navajonationparks.org, 8 A.M.–5 P.M.), where you can pick up permits for camping on the reservation, and the small **Navajo Nation Zoo and Botanical Park** (928/871-6574, www.navajozoo.org, 10 A.M.–4:30 P.M. Mon.–Sat., free), which houses animals injured or otherwise unfit for the wild. The collection includes a cougar, black bears, bobcats, and a pair of Mexican Gray Wolves. (Pets are not allowed.)

The headquarters of the Navajo tribal government encompass the tribe's executive offices and—attention, readers of Tony Hillerman's novels—police headquarters. The **Navajo Tribal Council Chambers** is an octagonal structure built of rock, representing a hogan. Depending on the council's schedule, you may be able to join a tour for a look inside at the log ceiling and colorful murals depicting Navajo history and daily life. Most council business is conducted in the Navajo language. To get there, take a right a half mile north of the intersection of SR 264 and IR 12.

Window Rock Tribal Park (8 A.M.–5 P.M. daily, free) centers around Tségháhoodzání (the "perforated rock"). This natural window is important as one of four sites where Navajo medicine men collect water for the Water Way ceremony, held to ensure abundant rainfall. The park is laid out in a quartered circle, the form of a medicine wheel, and features a veterans memorial honoring the many Navajos who served in the military. The graceful structure was designed with input from veterans and medicine men, and symbolism includes 16 steel pillars representing bayonets. The memorial includes a sanctuary for healing and reflection with a sandstone fountain and a statue that depicts a World War II Navajo Code Talker.

St. Michael's Mission, established in 1898, is now a museum (928/871-4171, 9 A.M.–5 P.M. Mon.–Fri., Memorial Day–Labor Day) documenting the work of Franciscan friars who taught school and catechism there.

Scenic Indian Route 12, also known as Diné Bíítah ("Among the People"), passes through Window Rock on its way north from I-40 to Tsaile. Tune the radio to KNNN 660 AM, sit back, and enjoy the views from the paved highway, which parallels gorgeous sandstone cliffs and softly rounded buttes edging small farms and ranches. Four miles north of Window Rock, **Fort Defiance** was where the Navajos' Long Walk began in 1864. The Episcopal Church built a hospital mission there in 1897, and the building was later used as an orphanage and boarding school. **Wheatfields Lake,** 40 miles north of Window Rock at the base of the Chuska Mountains, has areas for picnicking and camping. You can continue north, turning west at Tsaile for Canyon de Chelly, or take IR 134 through the forested **Chuska Mountains** to join U.S. 491, another scenic road that travels south to Gallup or north to Shiprock. (When traveling the reservation, stay on main roads and do not approach private property unless invited. Keep a watchful eye out for livestock.)

Shopping and Events

A large selection of traditional and contemporary jewelry, rugs, Western clothing, Pendleton blankets, and more awaits at the **Navajo Arts & Crafts Enterprises** store (928/871-4090 or 866/871-4095, www.go-navajo.com, 9 A.M.–5 P.M. Mon.–Fri) near the Navajo Nation Inn. NACE began as a craft guild in 1941, and artisans still buy supplies there. NACE also repairs and restores jewelry.

Thousands of people flock to **Navajo Nation Fair** (928/871-6478, www.navajonationfair.com), held early in September, for its rodeo, parade, music, exhibits, and pageantry. Held since 1938 to showcase Navajo agriculture and artistry, it's the largest Indian fair in North America.

Accommodations and Food

Most tourist activity in Window Rock centers around the **Quality Inn** (48 W. Hwy. 264, 928/871-4108 or 800/662-6189, www.explorenavajo.com, $90–100), a comfortable place with 56 rooms near the main intersection. The hotel's **Diné Restaurant** (all meals daily) is a local favorite, serving good food (plates $6 and up), including a breakfast buffet, burgers, Navajo tacos (of course), and mutton stew. Three miles west on SR 264 in St. Michaels, the Navajoland Inn (392 W. Hwy. 64, 928/871-5690, $70–90) has an indoor pool and spa. A handful of fast-food outlets are scattered along SR 264, from St. Michaels east across the border.

Hopi Reservation

The 1.5-million-acre Hopi reservation (pop. 7,000) is a cultural island surrounded by the larger Navajo reservation. Once, Hopi lands encompassed over 18 million acres, from the Grand Canyon east to the Lukachukai Mountains, and from Navajo Mountain to the southern edge of the Colorado Plateau. According to the Hopis' long oral history, when their ancestors emerged into this world, they were greeted by the earth god Maasau, who told them they would leave their footprints in many places before reuniting at the center of the universe.

A millennium ago, having left footprints in the form of ruined villages, rock art, and potsherds, the clans gathered at what are known today as the Hopi Mesas, three high, finger-like projections extending from Black Mesa. Surviving there—with less than 10 inches of annual rainfall and a 7,000-foot elevation—required cooperating with each other and with nature. Each arriving clan contributed

WHERE TO SHOP

There are two main options when it comes to purchasing native crafts (well, three, if you count paying five times as much at a boutique back home): buy directly from the artists themselves or buy from a trading post or gallery. Buying from the creator, either in his or her home or at a roadside or flea market stand, adds not only the personal touch but also the opportunity to get the best price. It helps to know what you're looking for in this situation and to have an idea of how to judge quality and a fair price. To be honest, a good number of items for sale at tourist spots like Monument Valley are mere trinkets. (But if something pleases you, why not buy it and enjoy it?)

Trading posts and galleries charge higher prices, and at an established post, you can be assured that you're getting a quality product, with the reputation of the store behind it. Employees are happy to let you browse and to lend their expert advice if necessary, and they can pack up and ship your purchases back home. Some off-reservation posts have pawn departments, and unredeemed goods (known as dead pawn) may be offered for sale or auction.

Wherever you buy an item, try to find out where and when it was made and ask for a **certificate of authenticity,** or else a receipt with the name and contact information of the artist or gallery, the artist's name and tribal affiliation, and the price, including the original price if you received a discount.

The **Indian Arts and Crafts Act of 1990** prohibits the misrepresentation of Native American arts and crafts (defined as a tribe member or artisan certified by a tribe) produced after 1935. For more information,

contact the Indian Arts & Crafts Board of the U.S. Department of the Interior (202/208-3773 or 888/278-3253, www.doi.gov/iacb).

The nonprofit **Indian Arts and Crafts Association** (505/265-9149, www.iaca.com) offers consumer tips and other information on their website.

© RICHARD MAYER

Richardson's, on Gallup's historic Route 66, is a prime example of a traditional post that has endured into the present.

ceremonies and married into other clans, creating community ties. Together, they became Hopituh Shinumo, the peaceful or well-mannered people.

Today Hopi life continues to center around a dozen villages scattered on or below the mesas. A few of the Hopi villages have been inhabited for over eight centuries. The mesas are quiet and isolated, and an almost tangible sense of tradition hangs in the clear air. Many Hopis

are farmers or artisans, and those with off-reservation wage jobs are likely to return there for weekends or ceremonies or to tend family fields below the mesas.

The Hopis welcome visitors, and they expect you to behave yourself. Unless you are in the company of a guide or local resident, stick to paved roads and village plazas. Don't wander down back alleys, particularly during ceremonies, and get permission from a village

TRADITIONAL HOPI ARTS AND CRAFTS

Ancestral Puebloans began making pottery when they settled in villages and raised crops that required long simmering, such as beans. The first pots were utilitarian, but as villages grew and skills became more specialized, pottery designs evolved and flourished. Today's Hopi **pottery,** still made by coiling and scraping and firing over an open flame, is exceptionally fine-walled, with intricate designs and a satin finish.

Hopi artisans also make woven, coiled, and plaited **baskets** from local materials such as sumac, rabbitbrush, yucca, or galleta grass. Coiled and wicker plaques are especially colorful, with kachina designs or geometrics. Basketry is made on all three mesas, and many baskets are used in ceremonies, such as traditional weddings or the basket dances marking the fall harvest.

Sikyatala, the first Hopi silversmith, learned his craft from artisans at the Zuni pueblo in the 1890s. Veterans returning from World War II developed the striking Hopi **overlay style,** in which a design is cut from a flat sheet of silver and set in front of another sheet that has been textured and oxidized until black. Hopi jewelry is marked with the artist's name, clan, or village, and the design may be pictorial or abstract. Gold and gemstones are sometimes used.

Kachina (katsina) dolls are some of the most distinctive souvenirs of the Southwest. Carved from cottonwood roots, kachina dolls were originally used to teach children about the spirit beings who live in the San Francisco Peaks and bring rain. When collectors began purchasing the dolls, carvers began making them with stands, sometimes depicting them in action. After the 1970s, when the use of migratory bird feathers was restricted, some carvers began to fashion feathers from wood, leading to astounding detail and craftsmanship. Sculpture-style dolls, often created from a single piece of wood, took artistry even further, with flowing forms and complex symbolism. Proving that everything old is new once again, a popular carving style today is based on the oldest of designs—the flat dolls first used in Hopi homes. Referred to as old-style or traditional, these kachina dolls are often embellished with feathers and natural mineral pigments.

Kachina dolls come in all sizes, and the quality of the carving and painting varies as widely as the price. Prime examples are true works of art and justifiably fetch thousands of dollars. Among the kachinas depicted as dolls are Mongwa, the Great Horned Owl; Angak'china, whose long, flowing hair represents rain; and the whimsical Koyemsi and Koshare clowns.

leader, or *kikmongwi,* if you plan on spending more than a few hours in any village. The tribe guards its privacy and traditions, so photography, videotaping, sketching, and any other methods of recording are *strictly* prohibited—no exceptions. Accept the fact that this is one part of your journey you'll have to recall from memory, because if you're caught breaking this rule, you will be asked to leave.

Early explorers arrived from the east; thus First, Second, and Third Mesa were named from east to west. The mesas are strung together by SR 264, and SR 87 travels north to Second Mesa from the town of Winslow and I-40. But no matter which route you take to get there, if you want to make the most of your visit, it's a good idea to begin in the middle, at the Cultural Center on top of Second Mesa, where you can arrange for a guided tour or find out about local events.

SECOND MESA

Of the three mesas, Second Mesa (pop. 800) extends the farthest south, offering commanding views. This mesa is home to the tribe's cultural center, as well as a number of galleries carrying coiled basketry (a Second Mesa specialty) and other types of Hopi arts and crafts. Three villages are located atop Second Mesa. To the northeast are Sipaulovi (shi-PALL-o-vee) and Mishongnovi (mi-SHONG-no-vee), located at the very top of the mesa beneath the twin stone pillars known as **Corn Rock.** Nearest the cultural center is **Shungopavi** (shon-GO-pah-vee) ("water place where reeds grow"). The largest of the Hopis' traditional villages, Shungopavi was relocated to the top of the mesa after the Pueblo Revolt of 1680, but its roots reach back to the mesas' very first settlement, established by the Bear Clan before the 1100s.

Sights and Tours

Along SR 264, west of its intersection with SR 87, the **Hopi Cultural Center** (928/734-2401, www.hopiculturalcenter.com) encompasses a motel and restaurant adjacent to a museum of Hopi crafts and interpretive displays (928/734-6650, 8 A.M.–5 P.M. Mon.–Fri., 9 A.M.–3 P.M. Sat. and Sun., $3 pp). While you're at the museum, be sure to try some traditional paper-thin *piki* bread, made with blue-corn flour and baked on top of a heated stone.

If you haven't made tour reservations prior to your arrival, you can find out about guided tours there. Traveling with a guide is the best—and in many cases the only—way to experience Hopi culture. No hiking is allowed without a guide, and visitors are prohibited from certain culturally sensitive areas. Guides are not only excellent sources of information but also gracious hosts who can help you avoid making well-intentioned but embarrassing blunders during your visit.

You may also directly contact guides, such as **Bertram Tsavadawa** (928/734-9544 or 928/306-7849, ancientpathways2004@yahoo.com) and **Gary Tso** (928/734-2567, lh-hunter58@hotmail.com), a katsina carver who can introduce you to Hopi artists and take you to their home studios. Professional anthropologist **Micah Loma'omvaya** (928/734-0230 or 928/734-9549, info@hopitours.com or hopianthro@yahoo.com) offers archaeological tours to ruins and other sites on the reservation, starting at $75 per person for a half day. For those arriving from the west, the Legacy Inn in Moenkopi (the westernmost Hopi village near Tuba City) can also arrange a variety of tours.

You'll need a guide if you want to see **Dawa Park** (also known as Taawaki), one of the most fascinating archaeological sites in the Southwest. Pecked or carved into the walls of this horseshoe-shaped canyon are thousands of petroglyphs, including animal- and human-like figures and spirals, which may represent the long migrations made by ancestral clans to the center place.

Sipaulovi (meaning "place of the mosquitoes") hosts hour-long village walking tours (reservations requested, $15 pp) beginning at the visitors center (928/737-5426, www.sipaulovihopiinformationcenter.org, 9 A.M.–4 P.M. Mon.–Fri.). To get there from the Hopi Cultural Center, go east on SR 264 to the second stop sign (just past milepost 379) and turn left onto a paved road, driving three miles to the visitors center, located in the heart of the village. General manager Bonnie Secakuku begins tours with a well-produced video about clan migrations and village history.

Shopping

Numerous galleries are scattered along the roads on Second Mesa, including **Sewukiwma's Arts & Crafts** (928/734-0388), east of the Cultural Center, and Alph Sekakuku's **Hopi Fine Arts** (928/737-2222), located at the base of Second Mesa, where SR 264 is joined by SR 87. East of the Cultural Center at milepost 381 you'll find Janice and Joseph Day's **Tsakurshovi** (928/734-2478), a fascinating store with an intriguing selection of Hopi and Navajo work, including many old-style katsina carvings. The Cultural Center may be the mesas' official center of tourism, but Tsakurshovi is an informal (and impeccable) source of information on everything from local artists to regional travel. The Days supply locals with ceremonial and art supplies, which explains the quantities of cottonwood root, turtle shells, furs, and herbs you'll see inside and outside the store.

Accommodations and Food

The **Cultural Center motel** (928/734-2401) has modest but clean rooms for $95–100 ($75–80 Oct.–Feb.). Camping is free—there are no hookups or amenities, but campers can access the public restrooms at the Cultural Center.

The **restaurant** (928/734-2402) serves all meals daily—inexpensive American food and local specialties such as fry bread made from blue corn or *nöqkwivi*, a traditional hominy-and-mutton stew. You may find it difficult to resist the tempting scents wafting across the road from the **Spider Grill.** Don't let appearances dissuade you from trying this local favorite—though currently served tarp-and-tailgate style, fajitas, burritos, and the like are fresh and tasty. The owners plan to build a permanent structure in the future. (An aside: Banks typically don't offer construction loans on the reservation, so enterprising locals start and finish projects as cash flow allows. Hence, you'll see many works in progress on the mesas.)

You'll find **Hilda Burger,** a popular village hangout, in nearby Shungopavi. At the SR 264/87 intersection is a gas station, **post office,** and **LKD's Diner,** serving breakfast and lunch Monday–Saturday in season; Monday–Friday otherwise.

THIRD MESA

The westernmost mesa is home to four villages—Kykotsmovi, Hotevilla, Bacavi, and Oraibi. Many katsina carvers live in these villages, but Third Mesa is also known for wicker basketry and other crafts. Oraibi is arguably the oldest continuously inhabited village in North America. (First Mesa's Walpi and Acoma in New Mexico also make persuasive claims for this title.) For a time, Old Oraibi was the largest village on the three mesas, but in 1906 internal strife split the community. "Friendlies" wanted to cooperate with the U.S. government's Bureau of Indian Affairs, while "Hostiles," led by a conservative villager named Youkeoma, refused. They settled the dispute with a pushing contest: A line was etched in the ground and the groups lined up on either side. At a signal, each started shoving. When the dust cleared, those friendly to the U.S. government had won, and Youkeoma led his people off to found Hotevilla. Third Mesa's youngest village was formed in 1907 by Hotevilla residents who wished to return to Oraibi. Their request was refused, so instead they founded Bacavi, "place of reeds."

Sights

Those who arrive at Third Mesa from the west will pass **Pumpkin Seed Point,** a picnic area with views of the **Hopi Buttes.** These dark, rocky volcanic necks are horizon markers used in the traditional Hopi ceremonial calendar. When the rising sun aligns with a particular point, it signals the appropriate time for events such as Powamuya, when seeds are sprouted inside kivas and handed out during a katsina procession known as the Bean Dance. This ceremony, like others, is layered with meaning. It heralds the growing season not only of crops but also of children, and some are initiated into katsina societies at this time.

At **Old Oraibi** (oh-RYE-bee), inhabited since the 12th century, past meets present in a windswept collection of stone and cinderblock homes. Near the line in the rock where village factions held a pushing contest to decide Oraibi's fate, an inscription reads, "Well it have to be this way now, that when you pass me over this LINE it will be DONE. Sept. 8, 1906."

Several guides offer walking tours of the village. If you choose to explore on your own, park outside the village or at **Hamana So-o's Arts and Crafts** (928/206-6392) and don't wander beyond the central plaza. Oraibi is not a movie set or a museum; be respectful of people's private property. A few residents sell crafts and food from their homes, and they advertise with signs posted in their windows. Look toward the south end of the mesa, where you'll see the ruins of an old Mennonite church, built in 1901 and destroyed by lightning (a second strike) in 1942, which may have pleased many of the village's traditional residents.

Shopping and Services

Third Mesa's largest community is **Kykotsmovi** (kee-KOTS-moh-vee), founded by residents of Old Oraibi near a spring at the mesa's base. Also known as New Oraibi or K-Town, Kykotsmovi (pop. 800) is the home of the modern Hopi government. The **Hopi Cultural Preservation Office** (1 Main St., 928/734-3612) provides visitor information out of the Tribal Headquarters building. Near the intersection of SR 264 and

IR 2, the **Kykotsmovi Village Store** offers sandwiches, pizzas, and other deli items.

A few miles northwest on SR 264 are the mostly residential villages of Hotevilla (HOAT-vih-lah) and Bacavi (BAH-kah-vee). There's a gas station in Hotevilla, considered the most conservative of the Hopi villages, and you may see signs on homes where artists have items for sale. Hotevilla is also the home of Hopi Radio (KUYI 88.1 FM), an enjoyable travel companion with a blend of national news and local programming that might include farming discussions or a teen show.

West of Kykotsmovi on the way to the turn-off to Oraibi, you'll find **Sockyma's Arts and Crafts** (928/734-6667), **Calnimptewa Gallery** (928/734-2406), and **Monongya Gallery** (928/734-2344), which has one of the largest selections of kachina carvings around. South on the Leupp (pronounced "Loop") Road, IR 2, is **Quotskuyva Fine Art and Gifts.**

IR 2 heads south from Kykotsmovi to Leupp and IR 15. From Leupp, IR 15 leads to Winona (of the Route 66 song), which is only a short distance from Flagstaff. This lovely, quiet drive between Flagstaff and Third Mesa is paved the entire way. A couple miles south of Kykotsmovi, just west of IR 2, the aptly named **Hungry Bear** restaurant (928/734-1239) serves hearty meals.

FIRST MESA

SR 264 winds around the base of First Mesa to **Polacca** (po-LAH-kah, "butterfly"). Many Hopi potters live there or in the three mesa-top villages, and you will likely see signs noting "potteries for sale." Most residents of Polacca, founded in 1890, are aligned with clans and societies from Hano, Sichomovi, or Walpi, the three older villages atop the mesa. Intersecting SR 264, a steep and narrow paved road climbs to the top of First Mesa, just over a mile. The road is suitable for passenger cars, but RVs and other large vehicles must be parked at the bottom.

The village at the edge of the mesa is **Hano,** founded by Tewa Indians from the Rio Grande pueblos. Fleeing the Spanish after the Pueblo Revolt of 1680, the Tewa were allowed to settle there by the Hopi if they agreed to guard access to the mesa. This was the home of the famous Hopi-Tewa potter Nampeyo, born in 1860, who based her designs on ancient pottery shards dug up by archaeologist Jesse Walter Fewkes. Thanks to the efforts of the Fred Harvey Company, which displayed her work at the Grand Canyon, she became famous and traveled around the country demonstrating her craft. Nampeyo eventually became blind, but her daughters learned her techniques and handed them down to the present generation. Just beyond Hano, **Sichomovi** (see-CHO-mo-vee) was founded in 1750 by residents of **Walpi** (WAHL-pee), the centuries-old village perched on the southernmost tip of the mesa.

Sights

Ponsi Hall (928/737-2670, 9 A.M.–3 P.M. Mon.–Sat.), located on the main road that enters the mesa-top villages, has a few parking spaces out front, and inside there are displays about Hopi culture. There you can join a **guided walking tour** ($13) that leads from Sichomovi through Walpi, which is otherwise closed to visitors. Walpi, meaning "the gap," refers to the narrow causeway of stone that isolates the tiny village almost completely from the rest of the mesa—and, it seems, from the modern age as well. The village, which dates back to A.D. 900 by some accounts, lacks running water and electricity. Only a few villagers live there today, but many others consider Walpi home, returning for special occasions such as the Snake Dance ceremony (closed to the public). With nothing but sky and stone in every direction, Walpi offers a striking panorama that has hardly changed over the centuries.

Shopping and Services

A few residents often bring crafts to sell on the steps of Ponsi Hall or along the route to Walpi. Several artists live in First Mesa villages, and you may note signs in windows or doorways indicating art for sale. In some cases, the quality is not equal to that offered by galleries and shops, but prices will be lower. Groups interested in having a traditional Hopi meal can make advance arrangements with First Mesa's administration services (928/737-2670).

At the base of First Mesa in Polacca, the Circle M convenience store has gas pumps. The Hopi Health Care Center (928/737-6000) is located along SR 264. Most days around noon, local cooks arrive at the picnic ramadas next to the parking lot with inexpensive (and tasty) burritos, sandwiches, turnovers, popcorn, and other treats still warm from the oven. You can put together a home-cooked meal for less than $5.

KEAMS CANYON

The natural oasis of **Keams Canyon,** called Pongsikya by the Hopi, was originally known to Anglo settlers as Peach Orchard Springs. This off-reservation town is named for Englishman Thomas Keam, once a trooper under Colonel Kit Carson (whose 1863 signature is inscribed on the canyon wall). Keam opened a trading post there in 1869 and married a Hopi woman. He quarreled with the Bureau of Indian Affairs superintendent, who demanded that the Hopi stop their ceremonies and send their children to the nearby BIA boarding school under threat of force. The superintendent was eventually dismissed.

Shopping and Services

Keams Canyon hosts tribal and federal offices in addition to a hospital, post office, and **Keam's Canyon Shopping Center.** The shopping center incorporates gas pumps, a grocery store, and a small café. **McGee's Indian Art Gallery** (928/738-2295, www.hopiart.com) is centered around Keam's original trading post, displaying an excellent selection of local crafts, particularly kachina carvings. Follow the road up Keams Wash 1.5 miles to a shelter on the west (left), marking the **Kit Carson inscription.**

EVENTS

Annual events include **foot races,** long a part of Hopi culture. Distance running is a skill that goes back to ancient times, when runners pursued game or traveled between fields and villages. Hopi runners were among those who alerted villages on the eve of the Pueblo Revolt of 1680. In the early 20th century, wage workers "commuted" between their mesa villages and jobs at the Grand Canyon or Flagstaff. Today foot races are held not only as part of certain ceremonies or celebrations but also to promote youth programs and traditional community values. The Oraibi 8K race, held each August, is open to runners of all abilities and ages. The Lewis Tewanima race, held in Shungopavi over Labor Day weekend, honors the 1912 Olympic silver medalist. The challenging Paatuwaqatsi relay climbs to the ancient village of Walpi each September.

Usually held on Columbus Day weekend at the Hopi Veterans Memorial Center (just off SR 264 about five miles east of Kykotsmovi), the Hopi Tuhisma **arts-and-crafts market** is a lively event combining food and entertainment with opportunities to meet carvers, silversmiths, potters, and other artists.

It is a privilege to be able to attend a Hopi **ceremony or dance.** Most social dances (such as the basket dances held each autumn) are open to non-Hopis, though some require a personal invitation from a tribe member. Many kachina dances, on the other hand, are closed to visitors. Each village may have a different open/closed policy regarding a particular ceremony. The Hopi Cultural Center on Second Mesa may be able to help you find out which are open to the public, and a village usually posts a sign at its entrance indicating whether a ceremony is open or closed.

When you attend a ceremony, be aware that you will be considered a part of the collective spiritual effort, so you should act and dress respectfully. This means no shorts, short skirts, or T-shirts, no loud talking, and no striding across the plaza to get a closer look at one of the dancers. (And it bears repeating: No recording of any kind, including photographs or note-taking.) Plaza and rooftop seating is reserved for family and friends. Stand or sit in non-reserved areas and don't block entries to the plaza or get in the way of the ceremonial procession. If you misbehave, you may be asked to leave, or—perhaps worse—you may be publicly schooled in manners by *koshares,* the clowns who serve as social police.

The Painted Desert and Route 66

As much a state of mind as it is a physiographic area, the Painted Desert extends in a narrow arc for about 160 miles from Cameron to the Petrified Forest, between the Little Colorado River and the Hopi tablelands. Encompassing nearly 100,000 acres, much of it on the Navajo reservation, the desert is named for the colorful buttes and badlands eroded from the late-Triassic Chinle Formation. The Navajo call it *halchíitah,* "among the colors."

Shades of gray, green, lavender, red, orange, and pink become vibrant at sunrise and sunset. Most of the soils were laid down as silt and volcanic ash, and are marked by clays that shrink and swell so much when they get wet and then dry out that hardly anything can grow. Reds, oranges, and pinks come from iron and aluminum oxides concentrated in slowly deposited sediments, while blues, grays, and purples are the results of rapid events, such as floods, that removed oxygen from the soils.

Rugged hills and mesas dotted with junipers continue past the Petrified Forest and Painted Desert to the southern end of the Defiance Plateau at the state line. Though this high, arid country looks empty and inhospitable, humans have passed through there for centuries. The southern edge of the Painted Desert is traversed by I-40, the same corridor once traveled by Route 66, before that by army trails, and before that by prehistoric Indian trade routes.

METEOR CRATER

About 50,000 years ago, a meteorite 150 feet across slammed into the Arizona plain at upwards of 30,000 mph, igniting an explosion more powerful than 20 million tons of TNT. The impact threw 175 million tons of stone into the atmosphere, uplifted the bedrock by 150 feet, and turned graphite into diamond at pressures of over 20 million pounds per square inch—and it left a really, *really* big hole in the ground. You can fit 20 football fields into the crater, which is 2.5 miles in circumference and deeper than the height of the Washington Monument. The crater was originally thought to be volcanic in origin, but the tireless research of Philadelphia mining engineer Daniel Barringer convinced the world otherwise, making this the first-proved meteor crater in the world.

Visiting Meteor Crater

The crater is six miles south of I-40, exit 233. The site is privately owned, and perched on its edge is a well-designed **visitors center** (928/289-5898 or 800/289-5898, www.meteorcrater.com, 7 A.M.–7 P.M. daily, 8 A.M.–5 P.M. mid-Sept.–Memorial Day, $15 adults, $8 children) with a widescreen theater, exhibits on astrogeology and space travel, a gift store, and a sandwich shop. Admission includes guided walks a third of a mile around the rim trail. On the crater floor, a dummy figure in a space suit provides a sense of scale; Apollo astronauts trained there before going to the moon. On the way there from the interstate you'll pass the **Meteor Crater RV Park** (928/289-4002 or 800/478-4002) with 71 sites ($30), a gas station, showers, laundry, Wi-Fi, and the Hole Enchilada restaurant.

WINSLOW

The town of Winslow had its beginnings in 1882 as a railroad stop near Sunset Crossing, one of the few places where wagon trains, soldiers, and other travelers could ford the sandy-bottomed Little Colorado River. Winslow hit its stride in the early 1900s, when cross-country traffic poured in off the new Route 66 and local ranchers shipped their stock out through the rail terminal. In 1930 the Fred Harvey Company opened La Posada, perhaps the prettiest of its regional-style hotels, where train travelers spent days or weeks, often exploring the area on the company's Indian Detours. That same year, Charles Lindberg flew to Winslow Airport, which he had designed as a stop between Chicago and Los Angeles.

Though once considered ideally situated for exploring the Grand Canyon and Indian

© METEOR CRATER, NORTHERN ARIZONA, USA

Meteor Crater is deeper than the height of the Washington Monument.

Country, the town declined when traffic began to pass by on the interstate. Still, you've heard of Winslow if you've ever listened the Eagles sing their hit "Take It Easy." Today Winslow (pop. 9,900) has a border-town ambience, with quiet streets and weathered historic brick buildings. The restoration of La Posada has injected a sense of vitality into the town, and a number of interesting sights are within day-trip distance.

Sights

The corner that Jackson Browne and Glenn Frey sang about is commemorated at the **Standin' on the Corner Park** at 2nd Street (old Route 66) and Kinsley Avenue. You can have your photo taken next to the statue of one of the Eagles holding a guitar, or the "girl, my Lord, in a flatbed Ford" painted in a two-story mural on the facing wall. This part of downtown plays up its Route 66 heritage, with shops offering everything from souvenirs to fine Navajo and Hopi arts and crafts.

The quirky **Old Trails Museum** (212 Kinsley St., 928/289-5861, www.oldtrailsmuseum.org,

11 A.M.–3 P.M. Tues.–Sat., free) is housed in a 1921 bank building nicknamed Winslow's attic. An interesting collection includes dinosaur bones, Route 66 memorabilia, prehistoric artifacts, and the still of a local moonshiner who lived to the age of 97 on a daily breakfast of black coffee, raw eggs, and a shot of his own firewater.

A couple of miles northeast of Winslow on the banks of the Little Colorado River is **Homolovi Ruins State Park** (928/289-4106, http://azstateparks.com, 8 A.M.–5 P.M. daily, $7 per car). The four main pueblo ruins were inhabited in the 13th and 14th centuries by ancestral Hopi clans who eventually migrated north to the three Hopi mesas. The Hopis refer to Ancestral Puebloans (or Anasazi) as Hisatsinom ("the Old Ones"), and Homolovi is part of the Hopis' vast homeland. More than 300 archaeological sites have been uncovered there, and three pueblos are open to the public, with short trails leading to the ruins. There's a visitors center and a 53-site campground that can accommodate RVs up to 83 feet long ($10–35). To get there, take I-40, exit 257 to

Highway 87, go north 1.3 miles to the entrance on the left, and then proceed another two miles to the visitors center.

For a drive-up view of the Painted Desert, continue northeast on SR 87 to milepost 360, where you'll find the **Little Painted Desert County Park** (daily, dawn–dusk). The park is small (660 acres), but it has picnic ramadas and big views from its overlook, particularly at the golden hours of sunrise and sunset.

South of Winslow at **Clear Creek,** you can swim, fish, or bring a canoe or kayak and paddle into deep, rocky Clear Creak Canyon. Free camping is available at McHood Park (928/289-5714), five miles from town. Take Route 87 south to Highway 99 and turn left.

Shopping and Events

Roadworks Gifts & Souvenirs (101 W. 2nd St., 928/289-5423) overlooks the Corner Park. This upstairs shop stocks every kind of Route 66 souvenir you can think of, plus a few hundred more, from books to bumper stickers. Look for the late Bob Waldmire's postcards and Route 66 map. His eccentric and detailed drawings are works of art.

If you're there in late September, don't miss the **"Standin' On the Corner" Festival,** with music, arts and crafts, an auction, and a car show.

In 2011 the Navajo tribe broke ground on nearby Twin Arrows Casino, its first gaming establishment in Arizona. (The tribe operates two casinos in New Mexico.) In addition to gaming and entertainment, the $150 million project will eventually include a hotel and golf course.

Accommodations and Food

Architect Mary Colter designed her masterpiece hotel **❰ La Posada** (303 E. 2nd St., 928/289-4366, www.laposada.org, $120–190) for the Fred Harvey Company in 1930. Built in the style of an old Spanish hacienda, the "Last Great Railroad Hotel" counted among its guests such luminaries as Albert Einstein, Howard Hughes, Dorothy Lamour, Harry Truman, and the Crown Prince of Japan. All trains between Chicago and Los Angeles stopped in Winslow, and so did planes before

better designs let them make the trip without refueling. When Route 66 traffic increased, the hotel's main entry shifted from the train tracks to face the highway. But after I-40 bypassed downtown Winslow, newer hotels sprang up along the freeway, and the railway turned La Posada into office space. The hotel was closed for 40 years and nearly razed before it was put on the historical preservation list and rescued from the wrecking ball in the late 1990s.

Thanks to the tireless efforts of owner Allan Affeldt and his wife, artist Tina Mion, La Posada is well on its way to recapturing its former glory. Suits of armor, religious icons, and Tina's large, intriguing paintings make up an eclectic art collection, and the hotel's gardens invite strolling. The **❰ Turquoise Room Restaurant** (928/289-2888, all meals daily) serves contemporary Southwest cuisine as well as recipes from the Harvey heyday of the 1930s, all presided over by a chef nominated for a James Beard award. Dishes ($18–35 for dinner) use local and sustainably raised ingredients such as Churro lamb. Next to the gracious foyer is a martini lounge, and the hotel boasts two gift shops offering everything from Spanish Colonial–style decorative items to Fred Harvey memorabilia and Indian art. This is a special place, well worth a stop if only for lunch.

Winslow has many inexpensive hotels, including a **Motel 6** (520 W. Desmond St., 928/289-9581, $60–70) and an **Econo Lodge** (1706 N. Park Dr., 928/289-4687, $50–130). The **Quality Inn** (1701 N. Park Dr., 928/289-4638, $70–100) has DJ's Restaurant and Lounge (928/289-3274, lunch and dinner Mon.–Sun., entrées $8–18) and an indoor pool.

Family-owned for a half century, the **Casa Blanca Café** (1201 E. 2nd St., 928/289-4191, lunch and dinner daily) serves authentic Mexican food every day of the week. Entrées are $6–16. You can grab a burger or burrito at **BoJo's Grill & Sports Club** (117 W. 2nd St. 928/289-0616, lunch and dinner daily) and settle down to watch the Arizona Diamondbacks play.

Information

The **Winslow Chamber of Commerce** (101 E.

Second St., 928/289-2434, www.winslowarizona.org, 8 A.M.–5 P.M. Mon.–Fri.) has maps, brochures, and souvenirs.

Getting There

Amtrak trains still stop twice daily in Winslow, but the station (next to La Posada on East 2nd St.) isn't staffed; call 800/872-7245 for information. **Greyhound** buses stop at McDonald's restaurant (1616 N. Park Dr., 928/289-5710).

HOLBROOK

Though it may seem tame today, Holbrook (pop. 5,400) was once the epitome of the wild and woolly West. This ranching center was founded with the arrival of the railroad in 1881. The second-largest outfit in the county, the Hashknife, was based nearby, where cowboys herded up to 60,000 cows and 2,000 horses across two million acres. A spread this size naturally attracted rustlers, and for a time Holbrook was known as the "town too tough for women and churches." Until 1914, this was the only county seat in the country without a house of worship, though there were plenty of saloons and soiled doves. In 1886 the Bucket of Blood Saloon earned its name due to a lead-filled poker disagreement involving a member of the notorious Dalton Gang. A year later, Holbrook was the site of one the deadliest events of the infamous Pleasant Valley War, a decade-long feud between cattlemen and sheepmen. During the gun battle, Sheriff Perry Owens (considered a bit of a dandy when he first arrived in Holbrook) single-handedly killed three members of the Cooper-Blevins gang and wounded a fourth.

Except for a couple of ghosts said to roam the old courthouse, Holbrook's dangerous characters are long gone, and the town is best known for its easy access to the Petrified Forest and the Navajo, Hopi, and Zuni reservations.

Sights

Holbrook's stately 1898 county courthouse has been turned into the **Navajo County Museum** (100 E. Arizona St., 928/524-6558, 9 A.M.–5 P.M. daily, free). Collections focus on

Holbrook's colorful Wild West past, and the walls of the claustrophobic jail downstairs are scrawled with prisoners' graffiti. On weekday evenings in summer, the courthouse lawn hosts Native American dances.

Though renamed and updated, the route of the Great Mother Road is marked by vintage signs and historic homes and businesses in Holbrook (Hopi Drive), Winslow (Second St.), and Joseph City (Main Street). More miles of **Old Route 66** have been preserved in Arizona than in any other state. To drive a segment of the original roadway and get a dose of road trip kitsch at the same time, leave I-40 west of Holbrook at exit 269 and head for the **Jackrabbit Trading Post** (a curio store), where you can saddle up on a larger-than-life rabbit. (The Jackrabbit sign may tug at your memory strands—it was used in the animated *Cars* and *Cars 2*.)

Archaeology buffs and historians can step back in time at the **Rock Art Ranch** (928/288-3260), located along Chevelon Canyon roughly 20 miles southwest of Holbrook. The privately owned ranch preserves one of the Southwest's largest concentrations of petroglyphs and a bunkhouse used by the storied Hashknife Cattle Company. The property remains a working ranch, and the owners are selective about visitors. Reservations are required, and directions to the ranch are given when the reservation is made. If you visit with a group, you can arrange for a horseback tour, roping demonstrations, and a chuckwagon dinner.

Entertainment and Events

Holbrook's **Old West Days** in June brings re-enactors, music, crafts, dancing, and bike and foot races. In September the **Navajo County Fair** arrives, and the **Christmas Parade of Lights** illuminates downtown the first Saturday in December. In January the **Hashknife Pony Express Ride** carries mail on horseback along the historic express route from Holbrook to Scottsdale. Riders hand off mailbags every couple of miles en route to the Scottsdale post office, where letters continue to their destinations via regular mail. Even if you can't be there to watch the annual ride, you can send a letter via pony express. Address and stamp the letter as you would normally; then mark the envelope "Via Pony Express" in the lower left-hand corner and enclose it in a second envelope addressed to Postmaster, Holbrook, AZ 86025. (Pony express mail must be received at the Holbrook post office before the January ride.)

Shopping

Nearby Petrified Forest National Park protects a mere 10 percent of the area's petrified wood. Though collection is illegal inside the park, private landowners in the Holbook area can sell their rainbow-colored treasures, and local rock shops offer a bounty of petrified wood, fossils, and other geological curiosities. A few stores are curiosities themselves, including the **Rainbow Rock Shop** (101 Navajo Blvd., 928/524-2384). Look for the herd of dinosaurs guarding its entrance near the train tracks.

Accommodations and Food

Hopi Drive and Navajo Boulevard are Holbrook's main commercial arteries, where you'll find most of the town's hotels and restaurants. The ◖ **Wigwam Motel** (811 W. Hopi Dr., 928/524-3048, www.galerie-kokopelli.com/wigwam, $52–58) looks like a classic car collection parked among a forest of big fake tepees. Built in the 1940s and now listed on the National Register of Historic Places, the wigwams still have their original furniture and all their Route 66 charm. **America's Best Inn** (2211 E. Navajo Blvd., 928/524-2654, $45–52) is another inexpensive option.

Along I-40, the **Travelodge** (2418 Navajo Blvd., 928/524-6815) has rooms in the $50–100 category, and rooms at the **Best Western Arizonian Inn** (2508 Navajo Blvd., 928/524-2611) are $75–125. A Good Sam park, the **OK RV Park** (1576 Roadrunner Rd., 928/524-3226, $29) has 136 sites. There's also a **KOA Kampground** (102 Hermosa Dr., 928/524-6689 or 800/562-3389, $23–35) with 208 sites.

Diner fare befitting Holbrook's location on Old Route 66 is what you'll find at **Joe & Aggie's Café** (120 W. Hopi Dr., 866/486-0021, all meals Mon.–Sat.). From the honey bottles for the sopapillas to the chicken-fried steak platters, Holbrook's oldest restaurant (since 1946) does Mexican and American road food. Sandwiches are $4–8, dinners $5–15, and breakfasts $5–10. **Mesa Italiana** (2318 E. Navajo Blvd., 928/524-6696, dinner daily, $9–20) serves traditional Italian dishes, pizza, and steak.

Information

The offices of the **Holbrook Chamber of Commerce** (100 E. Arizona St., 928/524-6558 or 800/524-2459, 9 A.M.–5 P.M. daily) are located in the old county courthouse.

Getting There

The local **Greyhound** stop (928/524-3832) is at the Circle K at 101 Mission Lane off Navajo Boulevard.

PETRIFIED FOREST NATIONAL PARK

This park, extending both north and south of the interstate, protects one of the world's largest and most colorful concentrations of petrified wood. The petrifaction process was so exact that in some trees the original cell structure is still clearly visible. A wealth of late-Triassic fossils, plus ruins and petroglyphs from 10,000 years of human habitation, complete the picture. This treasure trove of science and history was declared a national monument by President Theodore Roosevelt in 1906, and in 1962 it was designated a national park.

Over 200 million years ago, this sparse grassland was a lushly vegetated tropical river system, crawling with giant reptiles and fish-eating amphibians. Some of the first dinosaurs plodded among cycads, ferns, and early conifers. Huge trees, many up to 200 feet high, were uprooted by wind or old age and swept down into a vast floodplain and buried in silt and mud. Over time, silica-bearing groundwater seeped through the wood and replaced it, cell by cell, with silica. Different minerals tinted the silica a rainbow of brilliant colors. Erosion eventually exposed the fossilized logs in the hills and badlands of the Painted Desert. Native legends regarding the logs' origins are

Navajo legend says that petrified wood fragments are the bones of a monster slain by the Hero Twins.

even more colorful: Navajos consider the logs to be the bones of the giant Yeitso, killed by the Hero Twins, while the Pauite told how they were the arrow shafts of the god Shuav.

Visiting the Park

The park's backbone is a 28-mile drive arcing from I-40 (exit 311) to U.S. 180 east of Holbrook, connecting several fascinating sites, scenic overlooks, and short trails. Very few people venture off this road, but backpacking is permitted (with a free permit) in the colorful Petrified Forest National Desert Wilderness Area north of the interstate and near the Rainbow Forest area at the south end of the park.

At the northern end of the drive, the **Painted Desert Visitor Center** (928/524-6228, www. nps.gov/pefo, 8 A.M.–5 P.M. daily, 7 A.M.–7 P.M. in summer, $10 per vehicle) has an introductory video, bookstore, snack bar, restrooms, and general information on the park. Rangers lead tours and hikes year-round, and on summer

Saturdays, cultural demonstrations may feature dancers, weavers, silversmiths, carvers, or other artisans. For two weeks around the summer solstice (June 21), rangers guide visitors to a spiral petroglyph, where a shaft of sunlight marks the longest day of the year.

A short distance beyond the visitors center is the **Painted Desert Inn** (8 A.M.–5 P.M. daily), a National Historic Landmark that once lodged weary Route 66 travelers and is now a museum and bookstore. For a time, this was a Harvey House, and Mary Colter redesigned its interior, collaborating once again with artist Fred Kabotie, who painted murals depicting Hopi legends. Nearby, the old roadbed is visible, lined with telephone poles.

Across the interstate in the central portion of the park, you'll find **Puerco Pueblo** ruins and **Newspaper Rock** petroglyph site. The pueblo is believed to have been occupied twice, A.D. 1100–1200 and 1300–1400. **The Tepees** are cone-shaped rock formations. A short side road leads to **Blue Mesa,** with panoramic viewing points and a mile-long interpretive loop trail. Farther down the main road, **Agate Bridge** is a large petrified log spanning an eroded gully.

In the southern part of the park, you'll see the most striking examples of petrified wood. A trail starting near the Rainbow Forest Museum leads to the popular **Long Logs Trail** and **Agate House,** an eight-room structure built by ancient inhabitants entirely out of petrified wood, which has been partially restored. The **Rainbow Forest Museum** (8 A.M.–5 P.M. daily, extended hours in summer) displays astounding fossils. Behind the museum is the short **Giant Logs Trail,** true to its name—one stone trunk is nearly 10 feet across at the base. Across the road, **Fred Harvey's Curios and Fountain** sells souvenirs and snacks.

Warnings against stealing petrified wood are posted everywhere inside the park, but some people still violate federal law, even though plenty of specimens gathered from private lands (and thus legal) are for sale inside and outside the park. "Conscience wood" displays showcase pieces that guilt-ridden visitors have returned, often after a rash of mysteriously bad luck. Just outside the park's southern entrance are two places where those with acquisitive cravings can find beautiful petrified wood for sale: the **Petrified Forest Museum Gift Shop** (928/524-3470) and the **Crystal Forest Museum and Gifts** (928/524-3500). Both allow self-contained rigs to camp in their parking lots overnight at no charge, though purchases are appreciated.

www.moon.com

DESTINATIONS | ACTIVITIES | BLOGS | MAPS | BOOKS

MOON.COM is ready to help plan your next trip! Filled with fresh trip ideas and strategies, author interviews, informative travel blogs, a detailed map library, and descriptions of all the Moon guidebooks, Moon.com is all you need to get out and explore the world—or even places in your own backyard. While at Moon.com, sign up for our monthly e-newsletter for updates on new releases, travel tips, and expert advice from our on-the-go Moon authors. As always, when you travel with Moon, expect an experience that is uncommon and truly unique.

MAP SYMBOLS

▦	Expressway	◖	Highlight	✗	Airfield	⚲	Golf Course
▦	Primary Road	○	City/Town	✈	Airport	🅿	Parking Area
▦	Secondary Road	◉	State Capital	▲	Mountain	▰	Archaeological Site
▦	Unpaved Road	⊛	National Capital	✛	Unique Natural Feature	⌘	Church
------	Trail	★	Point of Interest				
....	Ferry	•	Accommodation	⚑	Waterfall	⛽	Gas Station
~~	Railroad	▾	Restaurant/Bar	▲	Park	◌	Glacier
▦	Pedestrian Walkway	▪	Other Location	⬙	Trailhead	▨	Mangrove
▦	Stairs	∆	Campground	✗	Skiing Area	▨	Reef
						▨	Swamp

CONVERSION TABLES

°C = (°F - 32) / 1.8
°F = (°C x 1.8) + 32
1 inch = 2.54 centimeters (cm)
1 foot = 0.304 meters (m)
1 yard = 0.914 meters
1 mile = 1.6093 kilometers (km)
1 km = 0.6214 miles
1 fathom = 1.8288 m
1 chain = 20.1168 m
1 furlong = 201.168 m
1 acre = 0.4047 hectares
1 sq km = 100 hectares
1 sq mile = 2.59 square km
1 ounce = 28.35 grams
1 pound = 0.4536 kilograms
1 short ton = 0.90718 metric ton
1 short ton = 2,000 pounds
1 long ton = 1.016 metric tons
1 long ton = 2,240 pounds
1 metric ton = 1,000 kilograms
1 quart = 0.94635 liters
1 US gallon = 3.7854 liters
1 Imperial gallon = 4.5459 liters
1 nautical mile = 1.852 km

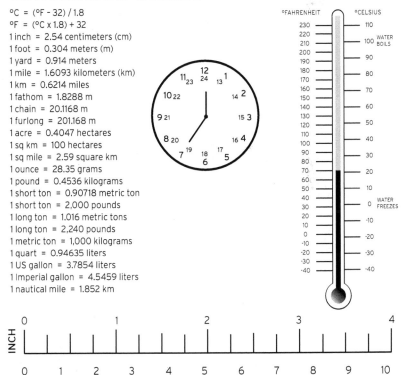

MOON SPOTLIGHT NAVAJO
& HOPI COUNTRY

Avalon Travel
a member of the Perseus Books Group
1700 Fourth Street
Berkeley, CA 94710, USA
www.moon.com

Editor and Series Manager: Kathryn Ettinger
Copy Editor: Jade Chan
Graphics Coordinator: Darren Alessi
Production Coordinator: Darren Alessi
Cover Designer: Darren Alessi
Map Editor: Albert Angulo
Cartographers: Chris Henrick, June Thammasnong,
  Kaitlin Jaffe, Claire Sarraillé

ISBN: 978-1-61238-155-8

Text © 2012 by Kathleen Bryant and Avalon Travel.
Maps © 2012 by Avalon Travel.
All rights reserved.

ABOUT THE AUTHOR

Kathleen Bryant

Kathleen Bryant was six months old when her parents bundled her up for her first road trip west, and she's been traveling ever since. Many of her favorite places are within the slickrock canyons and high deserts of the Four Corners, but her love for the region encompasses its cultures and cuisines as much as its landscapes. Starry skies, spicy food, rabbitbrush-lined roadways, and summer monsoon storms are some of the reasons why she's called the Southwest home for more than 20 years.

An avid hiker and history buff, Kathleen is particularly interested in Southwestern prehistory, a fascination that has taken her to places as diverse as the backcountry trails of Chaco Canyon and a lab classroom in which she scrubbed pottery shards with a toothbrush. She has also volunteered for the Forest Service, monitoring and stabilizing archaeological sites and leading visitors on tours of ruins and rock art.

Kathleen has written 11 books, including the award-winning children's story *Kokopelli's Gift* and the scenic guides *Sedona & Red Rock Country* and *Four Corners: Timeless Lands of the Southwest*. In writing *Western National Parks' Lodges Cookbook*, she combined her love of travel with recipes from historic park lodges. She has contributed stories to *American Archaeology, American Artist, Arizona Highways, Sunset*, and other magazines. In between writing her own books and articles, she has worked on numerous projects for other authors, from hiking guides and cookbooks to Tad Nichols's haunting tribute to a drowned canyon, *Glen Canyon: Images of a Lost World*.